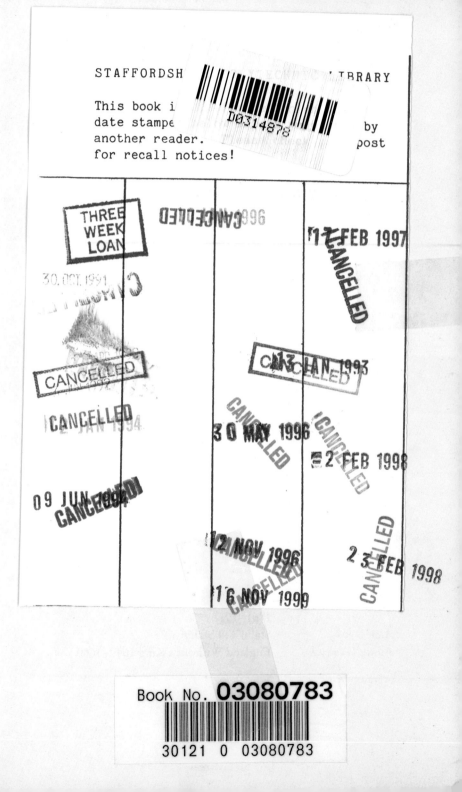

General Editors: Eric J. Evans and P. D. King

LANCASTER PAMPHLETS

Gladstone and the Liberal Party

Michael J. Winstanley

London and New York

First published 1990 by Routledge
11 New Fetter Lane,
London EC4P 4EE

Simultaneously published in the USA and Canada by Routledge
a division of Routledge, Chapman and Hall, Inc.
29 West 35th Street, New York, NY 10001

Filmset in Great Britain by
Rowland Phototypesetting Ltd,
Bury St Edmunds, Suffolk
and printed in Great Britain by
Clays Ltd, St Ives plc

British Library Cataloguing in Publication Data
Winstanley, Michael J.
Gladstone and the Liberal Party.
1. Great Britain. Gladstone, W. E.
(William Ewart), 1809–1898
I. Title
941.081092

Library of Congress Cataloging-in-Publication Data
Winstanley, Michael J., 1949–
Gladstone and the Liberal party / Michael J. Winstanley.
p. cm.—(Lancaster pamphlets)
Includes bibliographical references.
1. Gladstone, W. E. (William Ewart), 1809–1898.
2. Great Britain—Politics and government—1837–1901.
3. Liberal Party (Great Britain)—History—19th century.
I. Title. II. Series.
DA563.5.W53 1991
941.081'092—dc20 90-34969 CIP

ISBN 0-415-03574-0

Contents

Foreword

Lancaster Pamphlets offer concise and up-to-date accounts of major historical topics, primarily for the help of students preparing for Advanced Level examinations, though they should also be of value to those pursuing introductory courses in universities and other institutions of higher education. Without being all-embracing, their aims are to bring some of the central themes or problems confronting students and teachers into sharper focus than the textbook writer can hope to do; to provide the reader with some of the results of recent research which the textbook may not embody; and to stimulate thought about the whole interpretation of the topic under discussion.

At the end of this pamphlet is a list of works, most of them recent or fairly recent, which the writer considers most important for those who wish to study the subject further.

Chronological table of events

Ministries

	Prime Minister	Party
1830–4	Earl Grey (Nov. 30–July 34)	Whig
	Viscount Melbourne (July–Nov. 34)	
1834–5	Duke of Wellington (Nov.–Dec. 34)	Conservative*
	Sir Robert Peel (Dec. 34–April 35)	
1835–41	Viscount Melbourne	Whig
1841–6	Sir Robert Peel	Conservative
1846–52	Lord John Russell	Whig
1852	Earl of Derby (Feb.–Dec.)	Conservative*
1852–5	Earl of Aberdeen	Whig/Peelite
1855–8	Viscount Palmerston	Whig/Peelite
1858–9	Earl of Derby	Conservative*
1859–66	Viscount Palmerston	Liberal
	(June 59–Oct. 65)	
	Earl Russell	
1866–8	Earl of Derby (June 66–Feb. 68)	Conservative*
	Benjamin Disraeli (Feb.–Dec. 68)	
1868–74	William Gladstone	Liberal
1874–80	Benjamin Disraeli	Conservative
	(Earl of Beaconsfield from 1876)	
1880–5	William Gladstone	Liberal
1885–6	Marquis of Salisbury	Conservative†

1886	William Gladstone (Feb.–July)	Liberal
1886–92	Marquis of Salisbury	Conservative
1892–5	William Gladstone (Aug. 92–March 94)	Liberal†
	Earl of Rosebery (March 94–June 95)	
1895–1905	Marquis of Salisbury (June 95–July 1902)	Conservative
	A. J. Balfour (July 1902–Dec. 1905)	

*Minority Government
†Dependent on Irish Nationalist support for majority

Gladstone's political career

1829–31	at Oxford University; opposes parliamentary reform
1832	Reform Act; elected as MP for Newark
1834–5	Junior Lord of the Treasury, Dec. 34–Jan. 35; Under Secretary for War and the Colonies Jan.–April 35
1838	publishes *The State in its Relations with the Church*
1841–6	Peel's ministry: Board of Trade – Vice President, Sept. 41–May 43, President, 1843–Feb. 45 (resigns over Maynooth), Colonial Secretary, Dec. 45–June 46
1846–52	out of office
1847	elected as MP for Oxford University
1852–5	Aberdeen's ministry: Chancellor of the Exchequer
1855–9	out of office
1858	Lord High Commissioner for the Ionian Islands
1859–66	Palmerston's Liberal government: Chancellor of the Exchequer
1860	budget and Commercial Treaty with France
1861	budget and repeal of paper duties; Post Office Savings Act
1862	first public speaking tour of Newcastle and the North (Oct.)
1864	'pale of the constitution' speech on parliamentary franchise
1865	defeated at Oxford; elected as MP for S. Lancashire (July) death of Palmerston: Russell becomes Prime Minister (Oct.); Gladstone party leader in the Commons

1866	failure of Liberal Reform bill (May); government resigns (June)
1867	Second Reform Act passed by minority Conservative government establishes male household suffrage in the boroughs
1868	supports abolition of church rates
1868	defeated in S. W. Lancashire; elected as MP for Greenwich
1868–74	Prime Minister
1869	disestablishment of Irish (Anglican) Church
1870	Irish Land Act
1872	Secret Ballot
1873	defeat of Irish Universities bill; unsuccessful resignation
1873–4	Chancellor of the Exchequer (in addition to Prime Minister)
1874	Liberals lose election
1875	resigns leadership
1876	emerges from retirement to campaign against Bulgarian atrocities
1879	Midlothian campaign of public speeches
1880	elected as MP for Midlothian
1880–5	Prime Minister
1881	Irish Land Act
1882	Arrears Act
1883	Corrupt Practices Act
1884	Third Reform Act extends vote to rural householders
1885	Redistribution of Seats Act
1885	Gladstone announces support for Home Rule (Dec.)
1886	Gladstone's third ministry; Crofters' Act; Liberals' split over Home Rule leads to electoral defeat
1886–92	out of office
1892–4	Gladstone's fourth ministry, dependent on Irish support in parliament
1893	Home Rule bill defeated in the House of Lords
1894	resigns leadership and retires from parliamentary life
1898	death

1

Interpretations of Gladstone

Like the Colossus who bestrode Rhodes in the ancient world, William Ewart Gladstone (1809–98) straddled the Victorian era. It is impossible to ignore him. Yet, despite – or possibly because of – his voluminous diaries, correspondence, publications and speeches charting each agonising decision, each crisis of conscience, exaltation of the spirit and political calculation, the man still remains something of an enigma. With the exception of Morley's *Life of Gladstone* (1903), the 'lives' published around the turn of the century contribute little to our understanding, since so many were written by sycophantic admirers, and even subsequent attempts by historians to explain what motivated and sustained him have found that the sheer length and variety of his political career, stretching from 1832 to 1894, have precluded any easy generalisations. The publication in recent decades of his massive diaries, ably edited and annotated by distinguished scholars, has served largely to emphasise the personal and political complexities of the man. Perhaps, as an earlier disciple, F. W. Hirst, commented, 'A great man cannot be explained'. Perhaps, even, as a less enthusiastic historian has mischievously suggested, Gladstone was simply 'a middling bloke who wrote odd diaries'.*

*John Vincent, *The Sunday Times*, 7 November 1982

1

These diaries and the wealth of personal correspondence which has survived have certainly tended to give undue prominence in current works to Gladstone's own interpretation of his life and times. What we are often presented with is not the importance of Gladstone to the world, not even the world's view of Gladstone, but Gladstone's own view of the world and himself. This has done nothing to dispel the myth that the Liberal Party was 'Gladstone's' when in fact it wasn't. Similarly, tempting though it is to argue that he was the chief representative of the Victorian Age, personifying many of its values and contradictions, moving inexorably with, even moulding the forces which created it, passing away just as the old order was changing, there is also a danger of taking this too far. His colleagues were not in the habit of wandering the streets on 'benevolent nocturnal rambles' to *rescue* prostitutes. They did not – as far as we know – practise self-flagellation or spend their leisure time translating Greek texts or felling trees. They did not break into spontaneous prayer, or work sixteen hours a day or (thankfully perhaps) compile a soul-searching diary over seventy years or experience such a complex political conversion. Gladstone was far from the archetypal Victorian. Resort to stereotypes anyway, is always dangerous; the heterogeneity of Victorian society defies easy characterisation. In fact, like the Queen who gave her name to the period, Gladstone was something of an oddity by the standards of the time, a loner who neither fitted into nor represented any of its recognised social, political or religious groupings. Gladstone was very much his own man and, as we shall see, much of his political prominence and influence depended on his ambiguities, anomalies and persistent failure to conform.

For politically prominent he most certainly was. After entering parliament in 1832 as a young, unknown protectionist Tory he was to find himself a junior minister as early as 1834 during Peel's short-lived minority government. He then went on to serve in, and subsequently head, the Board of Trade and the Colonial Office during Peel's Conservative administration of 1841–6, rising to Chancellor of the Exchequer under Aberdeen (1852–5) and Palmerston (1859–66). By 1865 he was leader of the Liberal Party in the House of Commons, going on to hold the office of Prime Minister in the years 1868–74, 1880–5, 1886, and 1892–4. Even during his first 'retirement' between 1875 and 1880, when he gave up the party leadership but not his seat, he attracted more public attention than any of his colleagues. Yet his early experience as a Conservative protectionist and opponent of the Whig Reform Bill of 1832 was an unlikely background for the later leader of a party with a reputation for parliamentary reform and a commitment to free trade. Furthermore, whilst Liberalism became increasingly associated with the Nonconformist causes, Gladstone remained loyal to his High Anglican principles.

Before we can understand how and why this unlikely bond was cemented, how the partnership functioned, what it achieved and why it gradually disintegrated, we need to explore its constituent parts. Who were these 'Liberals' and to what extent are we justified in referring to them as a 'party' or wholehearted supporters of Gladstone? More immediately, what interpretations have been proffered to explain Gladstone's own political behaviour?

The man of God: politics as a religious crusade

Religion, or more precisely, Christianity, permeated every aspect of Gladstone's long life. It was, he declared dogmatically in 1839, 'the pole star of my existence'. Despite its neglect by John Morley in his classic biography, Gladstone's religious belief has often subsequently been put forward as the key to his public life.

Brought up in an Evangelical Anglican household, Gladstone went on to develop a sense of calling as a young man, particularly during his student days at Oxford, writing to his father in 1830 expressing a desire to enter holy orders. Although he soon abandoned this option, partly because of his father's less than enthusiastic response, both his private and his public lives continued to centre on religious devotion. He scoured the Old Testament for divine inspiration, compiled a meticulous diary accounting for all the time allocated to him on earth in preparation for the great audit with his maker on the day of reckoning, partook in daily private worship, mixed with and engaged in debate influential religious leaders of his age, and published on doctrinal controversies such as the Vatican decrees on infallibility. Even his loyal wife Catherine, whom he married in 1839, was bluntly, if sympathetically, told that the Church would always be his first love, his greatest source of inspiration and comfort.

3

The first thirteen years of his public life were characterised by an overt attempt to marry this religious fervour to practical politics. The power of the State was to be employed to correct the 'chronic malaise within the social and moral order' which Gladstone had identified. There was, in Perry Butler's words, 'an extraordinary sense of mission' running through this period of Gladstone's life; he was to be 'one of God's providential instruments in the divine regeneration of society'. Gladstone's means, expressed most cogently in his book on *The State in its Relations with the Church* (1839), was to restore, through state action, the privileges of the Established Anglican Church and reaffirm its indissoluble link with the State as the true and only expression of 'national religion'. He had little time for Protestant Nonconformity of whatever sect, and even less for Roman Catholicism and Judaism. He consequently supported the levying of church rates (compulsory local taxes to maintain Anglican establishment), opposed the removal of those civil disabilities which prevented Jews from sitting in parliament and holding political office, resisted the admission of Dissenters to the ancient universities and stood out against increases in state financial aid to, and control of, education. His belief in the Anglican Church's claim to unquestioned legitimacy and deference seemed unshakable.

In this he was at odds not only with the liberalising trends of the 1830s reflected in popular, militant Radicalism and mild Whig Reformism but also with the majority of the Tory Party whose adherence to Anglicanism was both lukewarm and tempered by the realities of practical politics. By appointing him to the Board of Trade in 1843, Peel, his mentor in more worldly matters, hoped to direct his energies to mundane affairs, but his ardour for religious concerns apparently remained undiminished. Until, that is, the 'Maynooth Crisis' of 1844–5 ended this extraordinarily reactionary phase of his life.

The Maynooth seminary in County Kildare had been established in 1795 to provide training for Irish Catholic priests. Both its foundation and its continued financial support depended on a British government well aware of the potential influence of the clergy over the population and the dangers of allowing them to become alienated from British rule, especially during the war-torn decades of the 1790s and 1800s. Annual grants continued to be renewed by parliament in an attempt to curry favour with the Irish Catholic com-

4

munity. As such, the policy already contravened Gladstone's strict Anglican ideals; the State was supporting a rival body to the Established Anglican Church of Ireland. The proposals of 1844 to increase financial aid and make it permanent were too much for Gladstone and he resigned his cabinet post in January 1845, much to Peel's incomprehension and frustration. Had he remained true to his original intentions his career would have been blighted. He would have remained a voice in the wilderness, fighting for a lost cause. But he didn't. After much soul-searching, Gladstone found a way of redefining his beliefs and objectives which enabled him to function even more effectively in public life. Not for the last time, principled pragmatism triumphed over hopeless idealism.

When the division in the House of Commons was taken in April 1845 Gladstone voted in favour of the motion. His closest associates were dumbfounded, seeing it as a gross act of betrayal. Some speculated that, like his sister Helen and confidants Newman and Manning, he was veering towards Rome. The experience was, he admitted, a 'nightmare', but he awoke from it with a new vision of his role which justified his continuing in political life for which he had now developed an appetite. Vestiges of his rigid High Anglicanism lingered: he spoke against the bill of 1849 which would have allowed a man to marry his deceased wife's sister and led the unsuccessful opposition to the Divorce bill of 1857 as contrary to divine law. For a quarter of a century he was also to fight proposals to abolish religious tests at Oxford University, for which he sat as MP between 1847 and 1865. But these battles only confirmed the conclusion he had arrived at in 1845: the State could no longer be trusted as the guardian of the Church and the latter ought, therefore, to be given 'greater autonomy' to pursue its own destiny. Indeed he became convinced that a tolerant, pluralist approach based on a belief in religious liberty was necessary to further the cause of religion and as a matter of 'social justice'.

Gladstone, however, carefully preserved a role for the State which justified his continuation in political life. As Richard Shannon has remarked in his recent biography, 'Abandoning office noisily was a way of quietly not abandoning politics'. He had already hinted to his Tory colleague Stanley in March 1844 that he thought 'the lower ends of a state ought to be fulfilled even when the higher ones become impractical'. Now he was to go further; government should

5

be dedicated to the pursuit of this 'social justice' and legislation was to be formulated according to a high moral code. While taking into account 'an equitable and comprehensive regard to the actual circumstances of the period and of the country' each measure was to be judged by criteria which stressed contributions to the material, the mental, but above all, the moral improvement of individuals, whether they be overseas or within the United Kingdom itself. It was his duty to remain in politics to ensure that this was the case.

For the rest of his life the notion that the State retained a high moral purpose in its management of domestic and foreign affairs remained Gladstone's guiding principle. His earlier commitment to specific causes or missions, however, was not dimmed. His espousal and single-minded pursuit of fiscal reform (see pp. 8–11) in the 1850s and 1860s cannot be understood other than as a 'financial mission' (Lord Aberdeen), dedicated not just to improving material welfare but to achieving social justice, furthering individual moral and political responsibility. In foreign affairs, he believed passionately in the 'mission of substituting the concert of nations for their conflicts' (1866), championing the creation of mutually beneficial links through trade while opposing military adventurism. His commitment to 'pacify Ireland' in 1868 was similarly subsequently described as a 'mission' and his strident denunciation in the late 1870s both of the atrocities committed on the Bulgarian Christians by the Turks and the Disraelian government's handling of the affair, had all the hallmarks of an Evangelical campaign . . . and more (see p. 65). Such dogmatic crusading, justified primarily on moral rather than material grounds, often betrayed an inflexibility of purpose, even, in his later years, an air of unreality and unworldliness which was to alienate sections of his party. Fortunately for Gladstone, however, his strident calls were echoed by a receptive political public for much of the mid-Victorian period.

The economist: architect of the minimalist state

The belief that good government was not only cheap but interfered as little as possible in the affairs of individuals gained increasing acceptance in the mid-nineteenth century. This is not to imply that there was complete consensus on the issue; battles over the role of government were hard fought at least until the 1850s and then emerged again with renewed ferocity from the 1880s as British self-confidence and superiority ebbed. Not all historians agree that what was professed was actually fully implemented, but most would agree with Eric Hobsbawm's remark that 'In the mid-nineteenth century British government came as near "laissez-faire" as practical in a modern state'. The achievement of this owed much to Gladstone.

Laissez-faire was manifested in three main ways. Firstly, the cost of government remained tiny. In monetary terms the amount spent by central government rose little in the half century after 1830 and even fell during Gladstone's period as Chancellor of the Exchequer between 1859 and 1866. As population rose dramatically over the century, the cost per head of managing the affairs of state did not rise until after 1880, while the proportion of the country's Gross National Product (GNP) absorbed by government exceeded 10 per cent only in times of military crisis (1855–8, 1860) and was otherwise rarely more than 7 per cent, a fraction of the figure which obtains today. Most expenditure was accounted for by military commitments and interest payments on the National Debt. Apart from Post Office employees and tax collectors, few civil servants were needed to perform the functions of government.

Secondly, alone among industrialising nations, British government dismantled the complex controls it had previously exercised over the economy. International trade was encouraged by the lifting of numerous import duties on a host of foodstuffs, raw materials and manufactured goods and by lifting bans on exports of machinery and capital. Legally sanctioned restrictive practices such as those which controlled adult males' wages and conditions of employment, had fallen into disuse long before the Statute of Artificers was formally repealed in 1813. Only women and children, who were not considered 'free agents' able to defend their interests in an unregulated, male dominated society, were afforded any legal protection from exploitation.

Finally, as a corollary of this, responsibility for social welfare was laid squarely at the door of individuals and their families. State aid, in the form of poor relief, was intended as a last resort and only the desperate were willing to accept the humiliating treatment which the Poor Law Amendment Act of 1834 enshrined in its policy of 'less eligibility'. The official view was that, since economic progress offered the opportunity for all to benefit and since inequalities could be removed by individual effort, pauperism was a manifestation of moral degeneracy, to be discouraged by making access to relief as unattractive as possible.

Gladstone strongly supported the principles which lay behind these policies and helped to create a climate in which they flourished, especially during his terms of office as Chancellor of the Exchequer. 'Economy', he confided in a letter to his brother Robertson in 1859, 'is the first and great article . . . in my financial creed'. As with religion, he applied the principle of economy to both his public and his private life. The financial parsimony or 'thrifty husbandry', as Morley commendingly calls it, which characterised his management of domestic affairs often appeared unhealthily obsessive. He regularly checked the price of his wife's household purchases, rigidly controlled allowances to members of his family, enthused in the 1870s about the saving of time and money which the recently introduced postcards facilitated, and re-used scraps of paper, even official baggage labels.

He applied the same detailed scrutiny to national accounts. 'The chancellor of the exchequer' he declared, 'should boldly uphold economy in detail. . . . He is ridiculed, no doubt, for what is called candle-ends and cheese-parings, but he is not worth his salt if he is not ready to save what are meant by candle-ends and cheese-parings in the cause of the country. . . . All excess in the public expenditure beyond the legitimate wants of the country is not only a pecuniary waste, but a great political, and above all a great moral evil'. Savings made by cutting salaries, reducing staffing or dictating the quality of paper and binders which government departments could use were small, however. Significant 'retrenchment', as the policy of reducing expenditure was known, could only be achieved by attacking the size of the National Debt and the policies of the major spending departments. Gladstone hoped to lower interest payments on the National Debt by reducing the amount that government borrowed each year. He also retained the income tax which Peel had introduced as a temporary measure in 1842, using the proceeds to pay off outstanding loans, and championed the establishment of the Post Office Savings Bank in 1861 to give the Treasury more independence from what he regarded as the grasping private banking system. Making significant spending cuts brought him into direct conflict with the

8

Admiralty and the War Office, the departments which, even in peacetime, regularly accounted for over one-third of total government expenditure, or over a half of annual outlay exclusive of debt charges. Whilst not denying the need for a military establishment, he deplored what he regarded as its unjustifiable extravagance and the way increases in wartime were generally financed by borrowing rather than through taxation, which would have brought home to the public the true cost of waging war. It was this desire to curb military expenditure which brought Gladstone into open conflict with Lord Palmerston, whose 'foreign blusterings' – notably the infamous Don Pacifico affair of 1850, his conduct of the Crimean War of 1854–6, provocative response to Chinese infringements of shipping rights which led to the Second Opium War of 1857, and support for increased defence spending during the French invasion scare of 1860 – Gladstone considered to be unjustifiably aggressive and potentially expensive. Disraeli's disregard for the principles of 'sound finance' during his ministry of 1874–80 occasioned yet more righteous indignation. Even in his last year in politics Gladstone was still stoutly denouncing the argument for increased naval estimates, this time to meet the German challenge. He had, he reminded parliament, 'uniformly opposed militarism' throughout his political career. It was on this issue that he finally resigned in 1894.

International peace and domestic prosperity could best be achieved, he maintained, by removing barriers to reciprocal trade between nations, thus encouraging economic interdependence and mutual self-interest. Although he was to become the most prominent proponent of this view, he was not its originator. The period of so-called 'Liberal-Toryism' of the 1820s witnessed the first tentative reductions in trade barriers, and Peel's administration of 1841–6 hastened the process, pushing through wide-ranging reductions in duties, particularly in the budget of 1842, and repealing the detested Corn Laws in 1846. It was only during this period that Gladstone became convinced of the virtues of economic liberalism and abandoned his protectionist views. Even then, his conversion arose from his administrative experience at the Board of Trade where he had discovered the illogical complexities of the tariff structure. Only later did he come to espouse the internationalist ideology of the free-trade movement which had been so eloquently expressed at the time by Richard Cobden and the Anti-Corn Law League. By

9

the time Peel's government fell apart over the issue of the repeal of the Corn Laws in 1846, however, Gladstone was firmly wedded to free-trade principles and found himself increasingly at odds with the rump of his old party.

When the Tories found themselves briefly in office in 1852, therefore, Gladstone executed a fierce demolition of Disraeli's budget proposals, which earned him a reputation as a man who understood financial matters. Consequently he was offered the post of Chancellor of the Exchequer in Lord Aberdeen's coalition government later that year and promptly set about completing Peel's work of tariff reform. His budget of 1853 lowered nearly 150 duties and abolished nearly 140 others. Subsequent budgets, especially in 1860 and 1861, virtually completed the process of abolishing protective duties designed to restrict imports; only a handful of specific revenue-earning impositions on non-essentials like tea and sugar were retained. At Cobden's suggestion and with his co-operation, Gladstone also negotiated the Commercial Treaty with France in 1860 under which both sides agreed to reduce or abolish tariffs on a wide range of goods 'to knit together in amity those two great nations, whose conflicts have so often shaken the world'. These years represent the high point of Gladstone's financial achievements and ensured that the doctrine of 'free trade' became indissolubly and causally linked with the rise of British economic prosperity.

Faced with possible cuts in government revenue from the reduction of tariffs, Gladstone found himself obliged to perpetuate income tax, first introduced in peacetime by Peel in 1842 as a supposedly temporary measure. (Pitt's imposition of 1799 had been lifted in 1816 after the Napoleonic Wars had ended.) Despite his constant reassurances that this direct tax would not be levied indefinitely, Gladstone had sound reasons for continuing it in the short term. Firstly, the revenue it brought in reduced the government's borrowing requirements; the budget surplus it helped to create even allowed existing debts to be paid off in good years. Secondly, the visibility of income tax in comparison with hidden indirect taxes would, argued Gladstone, act as a democratic check on extravagant expenditure if a situation could be engineered in which those who were entitled to vote were the same people who paid the tax. In 1853, recognising that some of the electorate were not taxpayers, and that they did not, therefore, have the incentive to vote for cheap government, he lowered the tax-free threshold on income from £150 p.a. to £100 p.a. and extended the tax to Ireland. Eleven years later he felt that the reverse was true, that increasing wage levels now meant that there were taxpayers without the vote. Consequently in an attempt to redress the imbalance and ensure that taxation and representation were inextricably linked, Gladstone espoused the cause of limited electoral reform, arguing for a lower property qualification for the parliamentary franchise. Thirdly, by adjusting the balance between indirect and direct taxation, Gladstone aimed to use budgetary policy to remove the inequity in the tax system which Radicals of the first half of the century had so vociferously condemned. 'Social justice' would be furthered by removing tariffs on the necessities of the poor; those who benefited most from rising prosperity would contribute more to the cost of the government which they elected. As Gladstone knew only too well, however, there were dangers in perpetuating income tax. The ease with which this 'colossal engine of finance' could be deployed to raise revenue might encourage spending. Moreover, the dream of utilising a taxpayer suffrage to provide a democratic check on excessive spending was smashed in 1867 by Disraeli's extension of the borough electorate to include all adult male householders, the vast majority of whom did not earn sufficient to pay income tax.

The corollary of Gladstone's reliance on fiscal policy and private initiatives to achieve domestic prosperity and harmony was a denial of the need for the state to introduce positive, welfare legislation. His supporters have been eager to stress, however, that this did not imply a lack of interest in social issues. According to Morley, Gladstone appreciated

> the social question in all its depth and breadth. . . . Tariff reform, adjustments of burdens, invincible repugnance to waste or profusion, accurate keeping and continuous scrutiny of accounts, substitution of a few good taxes for many bad ones . . . were directly associated in him with the amelioration of the hard lot of the toiling mass, and sprang from an ardent concern in improving human well-being, and raising the moral ideals of mankind.

But such beliefs justified out-of-hand rejection of requests for state interference in the labour market or for the provision of services.

'They are not your friends', asserted Gladstone in 1871 in response to criticism from a collier from Newcastle, 'but in fact your enemies who teach you to look to the legislature or the government for the radical removal of the evils which affect human life. . . . The only means which has been placed in my power of "raising the wages of colliers" has been by endeavouring to beat down all those restrictions upon trade which tend to reduce the price to be obtained for the product of their labour and to lower as much as may be the taxes on commodities which they may require for use or for consumption.' The maintenance of free trade and cheap government, therefore, was Gladstone's 'emancipating process' which provided workers with 'maximum employment' and 'the highest rate of remuneration for their labour'. Anything more was superfluous.

It followed from this that each individual had the opportunity and the responsibility to ensure that he/she achieved a satisfactory level of material welfare. Success symbolised moral worth and integrity and was to be accorded respect and recognition. Failure signified moral degeneracy, a lack of spirit, unhealthy dependence; it deserved little sympathy. Rather than relying on state aid, the poor were to be persuaded to help themselves. Not surprisingly, Gladstone was a life-long devotee of the principles embodied in the New Poor Law of 1834. As a young man he thought the Whigs had done themselves 'high honour' by introducing this reform which, he felt, rescued the 'English peasantry from the total loss of their independence'. Although in his old age he reluctantly consented to possible exceptions to the doctrine of social *laissez-faire*, such as the desirability of limiting miners' hours of work by law, he retained a dogmatic insistence that, in Sir George Murray's words, 'people knew better than the State how to make the most of their resources'. As an arch proponent of *laissez-faire* he played a major role in the construction and maintenance of the minimalist state and in portraying its virtues in moral as well as material terms. It was simply part of his mission.

This emphasis on individual freedom and responsibility together with a rigid adherence to an economic doctrine stressing free trade and cheap government comprised the greater part of what is usually called Gladstonian Liberalism. It was derived, not from a political philosophy, but from an amalgam of experiences, religious and administrative. It stressed liberty under the law but also its corollaries – responsibility and duty. The State's role was an emancipating one, enabling not providing, mediating not dictating, judging not accusing or defending, promoting the spiritual and material welfare of the nation as a whole, not the sectional interests of a class, caste or institution.

The constructive traditionalist

Liberty for all, however, did not imply power for all. Government was too important to be left to the whims of unfettered democracy. It could only be entrusted to the representatives of those people who were judged to be of sufficient moral worth to participate. At heart, in other words, Gladstone remained a social conservative and an unenthusiastic democrat, anxious to preserve the roles of a hereditary monarchy and aristocracy, to reaffirm the legitimacy of the State and Church, and to preserve a hierarchical social order. These traits prompted his Radical colleague Joseph Chamberlain to exclaim despairingly in 1881 that he was an 'impossible Tory'.

These beliefs are most clearly evident in his early years. At university he had thrown himself into organising an Oxford Anti-Reform Movement, opposing the 1832 bill as the work of 'Anti-Christ'. 'Birth, wealth and station, as well as talent and virtue, are among the natural elements of power and we must not war with nature's laws', he recorded in a memorandum later that year. Such views attracted the attention of arch-Tory the Duke of Newcastle, who obtained a parliamentary seat for him in the pocket borough of Newark in 1832. Even after it was clear that he would not lead the die-hards' opposition to Peel in 1845 over Maynooth, the Tories continued to woo him throughout the 1850s with promises of office and he could often be found entering the voting lobby with them. In old age, he continued to dumbfound friends with his reactionary views. 'Oh no', he thundered in 1878 when John Ruskin provocatively suggested that he believed in equality. 'I am a firm believer in the aristocratic principle – the rule of the best. I am an out and out inegalitarian.' 'I am for the old customs and against needless change', he was to write later, 'It is my singular fate to love the antiquities of our constitution much more than the average Tory of the present day.'

His views on parliamentary reform were slow to change. In 1848, with the Chartists apparently poised to renew their campaign for

13

universal suffrage, he enrolled as a special constable to preserve the peace. Eleven years later he was still stoutly defending the retention of pocket boroughs as a means of providing entry into parliament for members of aristocratic families, 'masters of civil wisdom' and 'calm, sagacious observers' who could provide valuable service to their country but were unlikely to survive the 'rough contact necessary in canvassing large bodies of electors'. His famous declaration in 1864 that 'every man who is not presumably incapacitated by some consideration of personal fitness, or political dangers, is morally entitled to come within the pale of the constitution' was hedged about with numerous qualifications. The Conservatives' extension of the suffrage to all adult male householders in 1867 was to him morally and politically indefensible. The secret ballot four years later he accepted with 'lingering reluctance'. The enfranchisement of women he viewed as dangerous and unnecessary. Re-immersed in the academic world of his youth in 1890, he told the fellows of All Souls College, Oxford, that none of the great reforms of the century would have been jeopardised by the existence of a more restricted franchise. His enduring principle had always been that the vote was not a right but a privilege, to be extended only to those members of society who could safely be trusted to use it wisely and rationally.

His private lifestyle, despite his religious devotions, often seemed closer to that of a hearty Tory squire than the self-denying Liberal Nonconformist with whose cause he is most commonly associated. He liked to eat well and could quaff a bottle of champagne even when dining alone. French wine he regarded as 'a most useful and valuable product', while he never faltered in his championing of the virtues of British beer, much to the chagrin of the temperance reformers in his party. Six months of every year he endeavoured to spend on the family's country estate at Hawarden in North Wales where he busied himself not only with intellectual pursuits but in taking an active squirearchical interest in its affairs and the lives of its inhabitants. Despite some reservations about the means that landowners employed to preserve their estates intact, he nevertheless confided in a letter to his son William in 1885 that he regarded it 'as a very high duty to labour for the conservation of estates and the permanence of the families in possession of them, as a principal source of our social strength and a large part of conservatism'. He believed strongly that

14

those with landed wealth were more suited by temperament and background to govern the country than men schooled in the harsher world of business. In his choice of colleagues he showed a predilection for 'men of station'; half of his fourteen-strong cabinet of 1880 were landed magnates despite their decreasing numerical significance within the party by that time – a proportion unmatched even by the Tory Lord Liverpool in 1812 or the Whiggish Lord Palmerston in 1859.

Hailing from a Liverpudlian mercantile background, however, Gladstone was always ill at ease in the company of the class he most admired, and they, in turn, held him at arm's length. 'There is something in the tone of his voice and his way of coming into the room', remarked Lady Eden to Lord Clarendon, 'that is not aristocratic.' As another Whig witheringly commented after hearing Gladstone deliver his budget speech of 1860 in his unmistakable provincial accent, 'Ah, Oxford on the surface, *but* Liverpool below'. For Gladstone, the importance of hereditary breeding and station was most eloquently and prominently displayed in the person of the Queen. Here, too, his poignant devotion and respect were not reciprocated. Although he was welcomed at court while Prince Albert was alive, from the late 1860s Victoria detested him with a venom to which it is difficult to do justice. In part this was a consequence of his party's pursuit of policies which she found deeply offensive, most notably the disestablishment of the Church of Ireland, the abolition of purchase in the army, a foreign policy which seemed designed to undermine British status and power overseas and, later, land reforms in Ireland and the commitment to Home Rule. Equally important, however, was the contrast between his approach to the monarch and that of the sycophantic Disraeli. 'He addresses me as if I were a public meeting', she complained after one audience with Gladstone. She would, she wrote petulantly to her secretary, Sir Henry Ponsonby, after the Liberal election victory of 1880, 'sooner *abdicate* than send for or have anything to do with that *half-mad fire-brand* who would soon ruin everything, and is a *Dictator*'. In the end she had to submit to the will of parliament, but relations remained strained, Gladstone being, in Philip Magnus's words, as 'incapable of making the necessary imaginative effort to understand and make allowance for the weakness of royalty as the Queen was incapable of making the intellectual effort to understand Gladstone'.

Yet Gladstone had never deviated from his open expressions of affection for the monarchy which he saw as the symbol of the hierarchical social order. He had no time for the Republican sympathisers in his party led by Sir Charles Dilke, who were incensed in the early 1870s by the Queen's continued refusal to appear in public or perform the ceremonies of state, and by the infamous profligacy of her son, the 'unemployed youth', the Prince of Wales. Instead, he sought to strengthen the institution of monarchy by, for example, entreating Victoria to curtail her trips to Balmoral and to perform the duties which her position demanded.

As the exhortation to the Queen to do her duty implies, however, Gladstone believed that individuals and institutions entrusted with the country's government and welfare had to act responsibly. Deference and respect had to be earned. This utilitarian traditionalism is best appreciated by referring to the country where Gladstone considered those in authority had reneged on their obligations: Ireland. In a letter to his friend Robert Phillimore in February 1865 he explained his decision to disestablish the Church of Ireland, to strip it of its legal and fiscal privileges, in the following terms:

I would treat the Irish Church, as a religious body, with the same respect and consideration as the Church of England, and would apply to it the same liberal policy as regards its freedom of action. But I am not loyal to it as an institution . . . I could not renew the votes and speeches of thirty years back. A quarter of a century of not only fair, but exceptionally fair trial, has wholly dispelled hopes to which they had relation; and I am bound to say, I look upon its present form of existence as no more favourable to religion, in any sense of the word, than it is to civil justice and the contentment and loyalty of Ireland.

The 'axe', he declaimed more vehemently in public three years later using one of his favourite analogies, had to be laid at the roots of this 'tall tree of noxious growth, lifting its head to Heaven and poisoning the atmosphere of the land so far as its shadow can extend'. Less enthusiastically he came to the conclusion that misconduct on the part of the landlords in Ireland, especially 'wanton eviction', was partly to blame for the apparent social and political unrest. Significantly, his first response to this perceived neglect of duty was to introduce the Irish Land Act of 1870, obliging landlords to maintain customary practices by recognising tenant rights; only in the very different circumstances of the 1880s did he reluctantly agree to legislative curbing of their powers.

A politician or a 'man in politics'?

Publicly and privately, Gladstone always insisted that he was simply 'a man in politics', inspired by lofty ideals, dedicated to doing 'much useful work'. He expressed incredulity at his popularity, and took offence at charges of opportunism and political calculation. He could affect an image of the innocent in politics, seemingly unaware of the implications of his innocuous actions. 'God knows I have not courted them', he remarked, apparently nonplussed by his sudden popularity amongst the working classes in the early 1860s. Contemporaries were often rather more critical of this affected naivety and unworldliness than subsequent historians who have tended to treat him as he would have wished to have been treated – as the great executive statesman, above the mean intrigues of party manoeuvrings, whose rise was due almost entirely to his unimpeachable qualities. Yet even Gladstone congratulated himself on occasionally possessing what he called a 'striking gift . . . in what may be termed appreciations of the general situation and its result . . . [and] for forming a public opinion and directing it to a particular end', and suggested that his espousal of Irish disestablishment in 1867 was one such occasion. Throughout his classic biography, however, Morley consistently defends Gladstone against the charge, as he sees it, that this amounted to 'opportunism'. The great man simply showed 'common sense'.

Even this clever sophistry, however, acknowledges Gladstone's political pragmatism. An acute awareness of the changing social and political order and driving ambition underpinned Gladstone's long career, saving it from premature curtailment in 1845, sustaining it for nearly half a century until, in old age, his sense of proportion and timing, as well as physical stamina, finally deserted him. No realistic explanation of his rise and long undisputed leadership of the loose federation which comprised the Liberal Party is possible without an appreciation of the extent to which public life and the pursuit of power intoxicated him. Despite professions of despair and recurrent expressions of his intention to resign, especially in the 1860s, he did not do so. 'The notion of a back bench', remarked Morley astutely, 'did not lodge itself in his mind for long'. Even in 'retirement' on the backbenches between 1875 and 1880 he simply could not abandon the public limelight for long; in 1896, two years after his final resignation and at the age of eighty-six, this phoenix could rise from the ashes and harangue mass meetings on the iniquities of the Armenian massacres, eclipsing his successor, Rosebery, who used the occasion to resign his own leadership.

Two qualities in particular sustained him in this career: pragmatism and, from the 1860s, publicity. He could put his idealism on the back burner until the time was 'ripe', until political success and its rewards were guaranteed. Concessions, even on what had previously been points of principle, could be justified, he explained in a letter to his son in 1865.

It is sometimes necessary in politics to make surrender of what, if not surrendered, will be wrested from us. And it is very wise, when a necessity of this kind is approaching, to anticipate it while it is yet a good way off; for then concession begets gratitude, and often brings a return.

It was, he continued, 'part of that business of reconciling the past with the new time and order'. But he was more than an astute pragmatist. He was a gifted political orator and operator, who was, in the words of an admiring opponent of the early 1880s, Lord Randolph Churchill, 'the greatest living master of the art of personal political advertisement'. From the 1860s Gladstone mastered the art of media politics, the first British politician to do so. By the 1870s his reputation as a folk hero, axe aloft, felling noxious and corrupt trees, seeking out and remedying injustices, was well established and lives on in popular historical imagination.

As the following chapters illustrate, the Liberal Party was only 'Gladstone's' because he strove to make it so. The rest of the explanation of his prominence can be understood only after we have appreciated both what the 'liberal' cause was and who subscribed to it, not only in parliament but in the country at large.

2
The Liberals

The date 6 June 1859 is often quoted as the day when the British 'Liberal Party' was 'formed'. The reality is far more complex.

The word itself – 'Liberal' – had been increasingly employed in political circles after the Napoleonic Wars, but as the phrase 'Liberal-Toryism' of the 1820s suggests, it was not monopolised by the Whigs, nor did it refer to a coherent set of ideas. By the 1830s it was not unusual to find some individuals variously described both by themselves and by others as Liberal, Whig or even Radical, depending upon the context. By the early 1840s voting in the House of Commons increasingly reflected broad party loyalties with men of these descriptions acting together against a reformed and revitalised Conservative Party under Sir Robert Peel.

Labels became both more and less straightforward after the Conservative Party broke up in 1846 over the contentious repeal of the Corn Laws. On the one hand some Peelites, ex-Tories who favoured freer trade, described themselves as 'Liberal Conservatives' but, increasingly, newly elected non-Tory MPs described themselves simply as 'Liberal', so much so that the old labels of Whig and Radical had virtually died out as political labels during elections by 1857 although both continued to be widely employed to denote political attitudes within parliament. But the increasing use of a common name did not imply the existence of a party structure or agreement on specific policies. Rather, the 1850s were characterised by fragile coalitions under the competing claims of individual leaders – Russell (1846–52), Aberdeen (1852–5), Palmerston (1855–8) – interspersed with minority Conservative administrations under the Earl of Derby in 1852 and 1859 which took office when these alliances temporarily fragmented. Politics, in Angus Hawkins's words, was 'a series of shifts and compromises that betrayed liberal impulses devoid of coherent purpose. . . . Party labels were useful for what they excluded as much as being guidelines to what was positively included'. As Gladstone himself commented in 1855, the 'great characteristic of this singular state of things is that political differences no longer lie between parties, but within parties'. After the rupture of 1846 he, like other Peelites, felt unable or unwilling to commit himself to any major grouping on a permanent basis.

The significance of the pact of June 1859 is that it sought to end this state of confusion. Whigs, Radicals and Peelites agreed to act together to effect the downfall of Derby's minority Tory government and Gladstone subsequently finally agreed to serve under Palmerston in the coalition government which replaced it. The June initiative, however, was essentially concerned with tactics within parliament. There was no intention of creating a nationally organised political party in the country. There was no national membership, no annual conference, no permanently employed staff and no regular income, funds being raised by *ad hoc* appeals at each election. Only with the creation of the National Liberal Federation in 1877 (see p. 60) did a structured mass party machine begin to emerge, and even then its membership and influence were limited. The chief characteristic of national party organisation in the mid-nineteenth century, concluded H. J. Hanham, was 'impotence'. Power was vested in the localities where associations and their leaders were 'sovereign authorities within their own domain, free to select virtually any candidate they wished'.

Who, then, were these Liberals? To what extent did they conform to the stereotype of the Nonconformist, northern businessman and to what extent did they share common values?

Parliamentary Liberals

The most noticeable difference between Liberals in parliament and their supporters in the country was social background. A property qualification for MPs, the absence of pay, and the time-consuming and expensive nature of political affairs combined to ensure that MPs were drawn exclusively from a small, wealthy section of society until 1874, when a handful of representatives sponsored by trade unions were returned. Defining the relative proportions drawn from land, manufacturing, commerce and the professions, however, is a more difficult task since individuals' activities do not always fit into the handy, mutually exclusive compartments devised by historians. Gladstone's own chequered social background, for example, defies simple categorisation: he had commercial origins, married into a landed family with income from minerals, yet retained a vocation more in line with the outlook of the clerical profession.

The ownership of land remained the most common characteristic of Liberal MPs until the 1880s (and of the entire House of Lords into the twentieth century). Few of these landed MPs, however, could claim any hereditary connections with the great Whig aristocratic families who had dominated eighteenth-century politics and who still expected, and were expected by many, to provide political leadership. John Vincent's pioneering study *The Formation of the British Liberal Party, 1857–68* suggested that in numerical terms such families were in fact a 'quite unimportant section of the House of Commons' by the 1860s, although as others – notably Terry Jenkins – have pointed out, Vincent's definition of Whig was unduly prescriptive. Both agree, however, that country gentlemen were heavily represented in the parliamentary party. Vincent enumerates 198 'great landowners' among the 456 Liberal MPs who sat for English constituencies between 1857 and 1874; Jenkins's figures for those returned in 1874 were fifty-five members of the titled, aristocratic families and forty-nine other great landowners or landed gentry, accounting for 43 per cent of the entire party (excluding Irish members).

Connections with the land were, however, even stronger than these bare figures suggest. All those with gross annual incomes from land of less than £2,000, those who just owned metropolitan property and those whose origins were unclear, were excluded from Vincent's category. Other groups in the party also had close links with the land. One quarter of Liberal MPs were relations of peers; over 10 per cent (forty-seven out of 456) were patrons of Anglican livings; nearly 20 per cent of businessmen and lawyers were also significant landowners and an indeterminate number were related to landowning families. On the front benches of the party, the substantial landowning class was even more overrepresented.

The average Liberal MP, therefore, was far from the archetypal northern industrialist, let alone textile manufacturer, of popular mythology. Such men, of course, did exist and, as the careers of John Bright, Richard Cobden, Samuel Morley, Titus Salt and W. R. Greg illustrate, they often achieved political and social eminence. But the 30–35 per cent of Liberal MPs with business connections were not drawn just from the ranks of the manufacturers. George Glyn, Gladstone's loyal Chief Whip, was a banker who had interests in railways; Derby's MP, Michael Bass, was a brewer; Grimsby's John Fildes was a Manchester stockbroker; William Rathbone was a Liverpool merchant. Those with direct textile connections were remarkably few. Even an archetypal cotton town like Oldham was represented in the 1850s and 1860s not by its cotton manufacturers but by James and John Platt, members of the local engineering family, and by a son of their father's original partner, J. T. Hibbert, who was also a qualified lawyer. The only cotton manufacturer to stand or be elected in the period was a free-trade Conservative. The local political arena was a more likely outlet for manufacturers' political ambitions. Here, power was personal and direct; involvement could be fitted around the daily management of a business, and it guaranteed a high profile and local esteem. A parliamentary career, on the other hand, offered much less and involved long absences from home, considerable personal expense and inconvenience and provided little opportunity to acquire real power, influence or prestige. Even when businessmen could be persuaded to offer themselves for election and were successful, their numerical representation in the House of Commons was restricted by the unequal distribution of seats. The industrial heartlands of the North and Midlands, especially the larger cities within them, remained seriously underrepresented until the Redistribution Act of 1885. Large-scale business representation was a feature of the late, not the mid-Victorian, period.

A professional career, however, could be more easily accommodated with political life, especially in the profitable world of the metropolitan law courts which, understandably, remained largely untouched by the reforming meritocratic zeal which was applied to other professions. About one-sixth of the membership of the Commons in the 1860s were lawyers and the overwhelming majority of these were barristers or QCs. Jenkins estimates that 23 per cent of Liberal MPs in 1874 were lawyers, at least one-third of them having connections with the landed class. This single profession continued to account for a similar proportion of the parliamentary party through to the next century.

It is difficult to appreciate the attraction of a political career for the majority of MPs. Few could ever hope to hold office and there appear to have been few direct material rewards. Vincent suspected that there was 'an atmosphere of search for private advantage' amongst the lawyers but could offer as proof only the circumstantial evidence that government created numerous opportunities for lawyers to obtain lucrative briefs which they could combine with private practice. For the landed Whigs political life was probably a combination of duty and pleasure, which could easily be worked in their extended sojourns in the capital. For yet others, like Gladstone, there was a sense of mission, one which has often been linked to militant Nonconformity.

RELIGIOUS AFFILIATION

In relation to its popularity in the country Dissent was grossly underrepresented in parliament. The precise numbers of Nonconformist MPs remain debatable, but the fact that the majority of Liberal MPs were Anglican is irrefutable. The year after the Religious Census of 1851 had revealed that nearly half of the country's religious attendances were in Protestant Nonconformist chapels, there were only an estimated thirty-eight MPs out of a house of 656 belonging to their denominations. Possibly as a result of the efforts by various pressure groups over the next decade and a half, this number gradually increased, but there were no more than sixty-four

23

Nonconformists among the 382 Liberal MPs who took their seats after the 1868 election.

Even these MPs did not reflect the relative popularity of various sects, as J. P. Parry's analysis of backbenchers who voted regularly on religious questions during the 1868–74 administration makes clear. Methodists of all persuasions, that is, members of the largest and most rapidly growing sect of the nineteenth century, were represented in the House by just three Wesleyans and one Calvinist. Primitive Methodists, those most closely linked with trade unionism and militant Liberalism in the constituencies, were totally absent. The numerous Congregationalists fared better with eleven MPs, but it was Old Dissent which enjoyed disproportionate representation with eleven Presbyterians, seven Quakers (excluding John Bright who took little part in the administration's religious controversies), and six Baptists. Most surprisingly, however, the largest block of MPs, seventeen in number, came from the tiny, socially exclusive, non-Evangelical Unitarian sect. 'Popular' Nonconformity, therefore, far from dominating the Liberal parliamentary representation, did not even dominate Nonconformist representation. In fact, the largest non-Anglican grouping was not Protestant at all. After 1847 the majority of Irish Liberal MPs were Roman Catholics. Their numbers were never less than thirty in the 1850s and 1860s and rose to thirty-six in 1868. The Liberals' increasing interest in Irish religious affairs during the 1860s, therefore, was not totally disinterested or dictated solely by Nonconformist pressure. Disestablishment of the Anglican Church in Ireland was an issue that bridged the gulf between these very different religious groupings and even offered the possibility that the Liberals might win back the Irish Presbyterian vote.

Mere listings of affiliation, of course, reveal nothing about the strength of individual commitment or the role of religion in moulding political activity. Most of the Catholic MPs were Irishmen and, perhaps for obvious logistical reasons, poor attenders, but they also remained relatively indifferent to many of the controversial religious issues of the day. 'Radicalism' was far from a Nonconformist monopoly. Richard Cobden, leading proponent of the individualist Manchester School of free-trade Liberalism, had Anglican origins, as did A. J. Mundella, a lace manufacturer who, with the Nonconformist hosiery manufacturer, Samuel Morley, was an active supporter of trade union rights. Many Nonconformists, however, were, in Parry's words, 'wealthy, complacent, established citizens' with little reforming zeal. Those who had this zeal, like the Unitarian Joseph Chamberlain, did not always draw their inspiration from religion. Within parliament, Nonconformists did not always vote as a bloc, even on questions related to religion. Of the fifty-nine who voted on the issue of secular education in 1870, for example, only seventeen were in favour. Baptists and Congregationalists provided most of the enthusiasm for moral and religious causes, a fact reflected in Edward Miall's leadership of the Liberation Society, but Quakers remained relatively indifferent to the issue of English disestablishment, only one of them taking an active interest. If Nonconformity did influence the party to any significant degree, then, it was through extra-parliamentary activity (pp. 30–3).

POLITICAL OUTLOOK

Only a minority of MPs exhibited that reforming impulse which is so often associated with the Liberal Party. These were, and are, most commonly referred to as 'Radicals', but estimates of their numbers vary according to the criteria employed. Among Liberal MPs in the period 1857–74, Vincent identified only thirty-four 'militant businessmen' with a 'sense of mission' and twenty 'Radicals' who were 'not capitalists or large employers of labour'; but his criteria for inclusion in these categories remain unclear. Parry, relying more overtly on voting figures for specific religious issues in the 1868–74 administration – disestablishment, secular education and 'other indications of radical feeling on religious questions' – puts the Radical figure much higher, at 115. Not surprisingly these 115 included the bulk of the Nonconformists (fifty); the remainder were university-trained intellectuals (nine), young Whig aristocrats (seven) and a mixture of businessmen and lawyers sitting for large borough seats or for Scottish and Welsh counties (forty-nine). But the employment of voting behaviour remains problematical, as Parry himself admits; we do not know how many of these men were responding to grass-roots pressure rather than acting out of personal commitment. Nor is it clear why attitudes to religion should be singled out for special emphasis in a search for 'Radicals'.

The difficulty in identifying 'Radicals' stems from the fact that

25

they lacked a distinctive outlook and did not always act in unison. In many respects they were simply 'active Liberals' who openly voiced what for many MPs were nothing more than vague sympathies and notions. Although they tended to share similar attitudes on questions related to the extension of the franchise, the rights of oppressed minorities, disestablishment, and the moral elevation of the individual, only a few, like Richard Cobden or John Stuart Mill, were capable of constructing coherent ideologies. Their cause amounted to little more than 'a miscellany of vaguely humanitarian enthusiasms, chiefly for the relief of the individual from metaphysical rather than material distress' (John Vincent), and they tended to diffuse their energies, becoming sections within the party, 'faddists' or 'impractical fanatics' selfishly dedicated to the single-minded pursuit of specific, narrow goals ignoring broader questions of party loyalty and balanced administration. James Stansfeld, MP for Halifax, for example, devoted much of his parliamentary career to obtaining the repeal of the Contagious Diseases Act which had set up officially inspected brothels in military towns. Edward Miall, who was secretary of the Liberation Society, dedicated to achieving the disestablishment of the Church of England, and Sir Wilfred Lawson, President of the UK Alliance for the Suppression of Liquor, were also specifically associated with single issues. Others, like A. J. Mundella and Samuel Morley, involved themselves equally in almost every cause, but concurrence on different issues did not necessarily imply that a collective identity existed. Yet others were concerned with what they perceived to be specifically regional concerns, especially in Wales and Ireland.

Such activists gave parliamentary Liberalism its reforming reputation but they also threatened to undermine its unity with uncomprising Radicals insisting that their issues be given legislative priority. Lacking a broadly-based view of government, they also lacked a recognised parliamentary spokesman, although John Bright had come by the 1860s to be accepted as their symbolic figurehead and Joseph Chamberlain after 1877 attempted to impose some discipline and organisation upon them. As a result, they were largely excluded from ministerial office. Bright's appointment as President of the Board of Trade in 1868 was a token gesture and only served to highlight his unsuitability for office while Chamberlain and Dilke both felt slighted by their treatment after the Liberal victory of 1880 when Gladstone awarded them only the junior posts of President of the Board of Trade and Under-Secretary at the Foreign Office, despite their prominent political profile. Radicals, therefore, may have endowed the Liberals with their reforming reputation but they lacked any broad conception of government and were unable to provide either the programme for, or the leadership of, their party.

Until the 1880s the majority of those who held ministerial office in Liberal administrations were drawn from the ranks of the landowners, especially those with Whig connections. Apart from Gladstone these were not particularly renowned for their espousal of Radical political views. The ageing Lord Palmerston had been a positive obstacle to reform, especially in fiscal and franchise matters, while his ebullient, patriotic popular foreign policy had more in common with jingoistic Toryism as Disraeli was quick to recognise. Lord John Russell, although favourably inclined to further parliamentary reform, lacked both the charisma and the energy to pursue wholesale change, while Hartington, the Duke of Devonshire's son, and party leader during Gladstone's temporary retirement of 1875–80, was widely acknowledged to be a political moderate.

The bulk of the party were what Vincent chooses to call 'Gentlemen of Liberal views' or 'the Plain', backbenchers 'who did not try to proselytize any brand of Liberalism' but 'professed . . . the accepted commonplaces of the country'. Backbench Whigs in this group differed from their colleagues only because they could trace their commitment to the pursuit of enlightened ideas of civil and religious liberty back to the Glorious Revolution of 1689. Only the successful 'Adullamite' revolt of 1866 against Gladstone's and Russell's parliamentary reform bill exhibited any clear evidence of them acting as a political group. Later unease in the 1880s about their party's attack on the rights of landownership, primarily in Ireland, and Gladstone's commitment to Home Rule in 1886 frightened many of them into permanent alliance with Conservatives as 'Liberal Unionists', but these deserters were not exclusively Whigs (see pp. 57–8). Deprived of the opportunity to hold office, unwilling or unable to arouse public excitement on any issue, the vast majority of Liberals remained and remain individually obscure, only significant collectively for their willingness or otherwise to pass though the voting lobby to support their leaders.

As implied above, the pact of 1859 did not involve a commitment to any specific policies. Despite attempts by pressure groups to oblige candidates to take pledges upon certain issues, prospective MPs were largely free to select and emphasise their own priorities. There was no manifesto or agreed platform on which all Liberals agreed to fight; Gladstone's rallying cries on Ireland, finance and Turkish atrocities in the elections after 1868 were no substitute for comprehensive policy statements. Views on fundamental issues like parliamentary reform ranged from Palmerston's and Lowe's downright hostility through to those who supported the implementation of the majority of the six points of the People's Charter which had attracted widespread working-class support in the late 1830s and early 1840s. 'Liberalism' was therefore both difficult to define and difficult to sustain. Questioned by the *Pall Mall Gazette*, as to the meaning of the term, over a quarter of a century later in 1885, leaders either declined to respond, arguing like Lord Shelborne (Robert Lowe) that 'no two people agree as to what liberalism is, or where it is to be found', or replied in terms which, like Gladstone's, suggested an attitude of mind, a moral outlook, rather than a coherent set of principles. This often boiled down to little more than a general belief in the capacity of individuals and society to 'improve' and make 'progress' towards some rational, enlightened utopia which, however, remained decidedly vague. There was general approval for the removal of restrictions on individual liberty and for the maintenance of free trade, while in the political arena there was an emphasis on cheap, accountable government and 'sound' financial administration. Much of this was expressed in negative terms, by reference to what Liberals opposed. Beyond that it is difficult to go.

Since it has proved difficult to define what 'Liberalism' was, it has been tempting to describe it by reference to what 'Liberals' *did*, or even more narrowly, by what Gladstone did. Such an approach is fraught with dangers. Liberals were far from being Gladstonian clones. John Stuart Mill's description of the party in 1865 as a 'broad church' was an appropriate one, implying both a loose organisation and the freedom of individuals to pursue their own causes. This was both the party's strength and its weakness. On the one hand it allowed a wide variety of opinions to be embraced; on the other, it guaranteed that there would be frequent internal dissension. It was this flexibility and looseness of purpose which allowed Gladstone first to join the Liberals and then to impose his own personal brand of Liberalism – his own crusades – upon them. As will become clear, however, it would be misleading to infer from the recurrent use of broad terms like 'Gladstonian Liberalism' that there was anything like an agreed ideological consensus.

Popular Liberalism

Parliamentary Liberalism did not exist in a vacuum. Public opinion, exercised through the ballot box, pressure-group activity and the popular press, was a major determinant of the party's legislative priorities. This pressure was not constant over time. It was not evenly distributed over the country or between social classes, nor did it always speak with one voice. All this made the politicians' task difficult. As the electorate grew larger, new interest groups emerged and the press assumed greater importance and sophistication, the ability to interpret, respond to, mobilise, even mould this mass support became ever more crucial, the rewards correspondingly higher. Reputations, as Gladstone well knew, were increasingly made away from Westminster.

SPATIAL DISTRIBUTION

Apart from London itself, the Liberals never penetrated the Tory heartlands in the Home Counties sufficiently to win more than a small fraction of the seats there. Their strength lay rather in the North, the Midlands, Wales, Scotland and, until the 1870s, Ireland (see Appendix). Only once between 1857 and 1885, in the disastrous election of 1874, did they fail to win a majority of English seats, but their superiority was never particularly marked, and they obtained only 57 per cent at their peak in 1857. Throughout the 1860s their lead over the Conservatives in England never amounted to much more than two dozen seats. This was largely due to their failure to make inroads into the county seats. Only once, in 1857, did they win more than a third of these; in 1874 their tally fell to twenty-seven out of 172, a mere 15.6 per cent. Their strongholds lay in the underrepresented boroughs of the North and the Midlands, especially the larger industrial and commercial centres, although even here there were marked local variations. Lancashire's reputation as a

29

Liberal county, for example, was largely based on results in and around Manchester; the political scales elsewhere in the county were much more evenly balanced while Liverpool, after a brief flirtation with Liberalism in the 1840s, remained resolutely Tory throughout the nineteenth century.

The huge parliamentary majorities which the Liberals enjoyed at their peak were largely due to the support of the Celtic nationalities. Only once, before the rise of Home Rulers in the 1870s, was their Irish supremacy challenged by the Tories. This was in 1859, and their surprise defeat did much to concentrate Liberal minds on Ireland in the subsequent decade. Between 1832 and 1865, Wales gradually changed from being predominantly Tory to overwhelmingly Liberal, a position it was to retain for the rest of the century. It was in Scotland, however, that the Liberals' position appeared most unassailable. At their peak, in 1865, they were victorious in fifty-two of the sixty seats. Even when they were outnumbered 3:2 in England in 1874, Liberals still romped home ahead elsewhere in the United Kingdom so it is not surprising that they continued to give so much attention to the concerns of regional nationalities. Throughout the second half of the century they were always much more of a British than an English political force.

It is tempting to explain such variations in support by reference to religion, agreeing with Gladstone's famous comment of 1877 that 'Nonconformity supplies the backbone of English Liberalism' and, he might have added, that of Wales and Scotland as well. Evidence of links between Nonconformity and Liberalism in the country is much stronger than it is in parliament. Dissenting clerics almost to a man voted Liberal and rare case studies, like Trevor Mcdonald's of Poole, which have sought to explore the impact of religion on electoral behaviour, strongly suggest that laymen exhibited a similar tendency, over 82 per cent of Poole's Nonconformists voting Liberal in 1859.

Militant Nonconformity also supplied much of the party's crusading zeal and organisational structure. Three pressure groups in particular have attracted historical attention. The Liberation Society (1853) grew out of an earlier Anti-State Church Association of 1844.

Under the leadership of a Congregationalist minister, Edward Miall, it relentlessly called for the disestablishment of the Anglican Church in Britain, that is, the removal of privileges such as the right of bishops to sit as members of the House of Lords and the Church's income from tithes and church rates. Unlike the Liberal Party, the Liberation Society had a central council and local committees dealing with electoral affairs. It also employed paid agents and lecturers, sought to influence the choice or platform of Liberal candidates, actively encouraged registration of voters and published its own official newspaper, *The Liberator* (1855), as well as receiving support from Miall's earlier journal, *The Nonconformist*. The Liberals' unexpectedly good results in the English counties in 1857 have been attributed to the intervention of the society and the flurry of legislative activity in the 1860s – notably the abolition of church rates in 1868 and the disestablishment of the Anglican Church in Ireland the year after – have been attributed to the pressure it brought to bear on MPs.

Leaders and supporters of the United Kingdom Alliance (1853) were also overwhelmingly Dissenters; indeed, there was a considerable overlap of membership with the Liberation Society. A temperance organisation, the UK Alliance, was dedicated after 1864 to the pursuit of the local option, that is, the right of ratepayers to veto the granting of licences for public houses in their area. With a staff of thirty, an annual income in excess of £13,000, its own weekly newspaper (*Alliance News*) with a circulation of 25,000, and the ability to raise petitions with more than one million signatures, the Alliance was a powerful organisation and it was difficult for Liberal leaders not to take some notice of its demands. Third, there was the National Education League. Formed in Birmingham in 1869 but carrying on the tradition of earlier societies committed to achieving universal free, national secular education, this enjoyed a rapid rise, claiming a hundred branches, an annual income in excess of £6,000 and a newsletter with a circulation in excess of 20,000. This, too, drew heavily on Nonconformist support, especially in the North and the Midlands.

Yet the relationship between Nonconformity and Liberalism remains problematical. Pressure groups' attempts to influence legislation enjoyed only partial success. Between 1871 and 1873, Miall's three motions calling for disestablishment received only eighty-nine, ninety-four and sixty-one votes, respectively. The local option was not included in the Licensing Act of 1872. Forsters' Education Act of 1870 fell far short of the League's demand for compulsory, state-supported secular education and left Anglican schools intact, even subsidised to a small extent by the ability of poor parents to claim assistance from the rates to pay fees. The weakness of organised Nonconformity's hold over the electorate was vividly illustrated in the 'Nonconformist Revolt' in the 1874 election which was intended to force Liberal parliamentary candidates to pledge their support for far-reaching reforms. Despite high-profile press coverage, the institutional support of the chapels and expensive leafleting, this attempt at concerted electoral blackmail was a dismal failure. Electors remained steadfastly indifferent to propaganda which emphasised abstract principles when to all intents and purposes the most glaring practical grievances had been effectively removed. Nonconformists were by then no longer legally discriminated against in any civil or fiscal way, the legal requirement to pay church rates had been removed in 1868, and the ancient universities had finally been obliged to open their doors to Dissenting staff in 1871.

The Religious Census of 1851 also suggests that the correlation between Liberal heartlands and Nonconformist strongholds was far from obvious outside Wales and Scotland. In the chief manufacturing districts and London, the majority of the population remained unmoved by the appeal of any religious sect. Paradoxically, Nonconformist indices of attendance were consistently higher in many of the counties which were never out of Tory control. In Ireland the situation was even more complicated. Here it was the Catholics who were overwhelmingly (95 per cent) Liberal in the 1850s; Presbyterians, especially in the southern counties, voted predominantly Tory (75 per cent). There would appear to be a twofold explanation of this apparent paradox. First, Liberal voters everywhere identified themselves more readily as *opponents* of the established Anglican landed settlement, than as active supporters of Nonconformist causes. What allowed them to dominate in areas where Nonconformity was poorly represented was the even greater weakness of Anglicanism whose strongholds were mainly in the south and east of England. Secondly, prior to 1867, the *petit bourgeois* groups – shopkeepers, independent producers, craftsmen, small farmers – who were the most loyal supporters of Dissent, were also the largest social groups in the electorate. However, whether their voting behaviour was influenced by their religion is another question. It is quite possible that their Nonconformist tendencies and Liberal leanings were both determined by their position in society. To explore this further we need to understand the nature of the Liberal electorate.

THE MID-VICTORIAN LIBERAL VOTER

The survival of pollbooks, published records of how individual electors cast their votes, have enabled historians to document fairly well the composition and political affiliations of the pre-1867 electorate. This, of course, was far from representative of the adult male population, the vote being restricted to £10 householders in the boroughs and forty-shilling freeholders and £50 tenants in the counties. Both Nossiter and Vincent have described the borough electorate as 'pre-industrial', pointing to the underrepresentation of large-scale manufacturing concerns and their workforces. As economic historians are increasingly emphasising, however, industrial growth in most of the country continued to be fuelled by expanding numbers of small or medium-sized businesses well into the late nineteenth century. Retailing, for example, was the domain of the individual shopkeeper while many consumer goods and services were provided by independent artisans. Since it was these groups which comprised the bulk of the new 'middle class' created by the industrial revolution and it was they who formed the largest groups in the post-1832 urban electorate it is difficult to see this as a 'pre-industrial' franchise.

Although the precise level of their support varied over the country, shopkeepers and artisans were usually the most Liberal groups in almost every constituency between 1832 and 1872. This was as true of textile-dominated towns like Rochdale, Oldham and Stockport as it was of the commercial cities, the market towns and even the counties which continued to return Conservative candidates for most of the period. Their ability to determine the outcome of an election depended not so much on the varying level of their commitment but on the relative size of other, more Tory-inclined social groups in each constituency. In the counties they were usually

33

heavily outvoted by the solid ranks of tenant farmers; in predominantly urban areas they were often able to carry the day, far outnumbering the ranks of less politically partisan professionals, gentlemen and larger manufacturers.

Their commitment to Liberal causes was long-standing. Recent analyses of the Wilkite parliamentary reform movement of the 1760s show that these 'middling sorts' were its staunchest supporters. Artisans had formed the backbone of the London and provincial Corresponding Societies of the 1790s; shopkeepers had provided the electoral support for the Radical Francis Burdett in the 1800s; many were active in the political unions of the Reform Bill crisis, went on to support Radical candidates in the ensuing elections, and provided steady if moderate leadership of Chartism in areas as diverse as the heavily industrialised North-East and the market towns of Essex and Suffolk. It was they who had packed the local vestries in the 1830s to spearhead the attack on church rates and had provided the most solid support for the reform of municipal government; Cobden's campaign for the incorporation of Manchester after 1838, for example, had deliberately focused on the city's shopkeepers. These men, in other words, were not floating voters or late converts to Liberalism, won over by Gladstone's wooing. They were the backbone of the movement.

Documenting this popular Liberalism is one thing; explaining it is another. Since these social groups' Liberal tendencies were exhibited on a national scale and over an extended period, usually irrespective of the dominant political climate, both straightforward bribery and the so-called practice of 'exclusive dealing' (threatening shopkeepers with loss of trade unless they voted in line with customers' preferences) can be discounted as possible major influences. These men represented what Nossiter has labelled 'the politics of individualism'. Their voting was neither an expression of deference nor the consequence of influence, but a free expression of political commitment. But a commitment to what – ideals, self-interest, or a fortuitous combination of the two? Sources are remarkably unhelpful on this crucial issue and historians understandably vague and unsure of themselves. Vincent's explanation, which has not been seriously challenged, stresses their disinterestedness; it was 'before all else the way these people looked at things, their domestic morality writ large'.

What they could hope for from politics was not improvement of condition or satisfaction of antipathies, but a sense of their own audacity and shrewdness, a feeling of participation in a demonstrably superior cause. . . . Liberalism did nothing to solve the problems of personal security for these people. . . . The canons of Peelite administration might as well have been applied to another planet for all the provinces knew of them. If people in Sheffield were affected at all by competitive examinations for the Civil Service or abolition of purchase in the army, it was through their sense of justice, not of interest. . . .

The prevalence of Nonconformity among these social groups has also tended to strengthen the view that ideals and values were paramount.

But the battle against an unrepresentative, unaccountable, aristocratic, protectionist Anglican establishment offered more in the way of returns than a visceral thrill or spiritual uplift. It held out the prospect of improvement in individuals' material circumstances. As the franchise reformers of the first half of the century had constantly argued, 'excessive taxation' was the result of a corrupt, protectionist, militarist state. The democratisation of government would, they hoped, bring an end to this situation. The removal of barriers to international trade did not just benefit the export-orientated manufacturers who have been most commonly associated with the free-trade movement. Consumers also benefited from the introduction of free trade, sound, accountable administration and reduced taxes. Since these 'middling sorts' were the chief beneficiaries of the rising standard of living in urban Britain it is possible that their political outlook reflected a sense of consumer consciousness. As consumers they had a direct interest in reducing the State's early nineteenth-century reliance on tariffs which were effectively indirect taxes on spending. The ensuing reduction in the cost of a wide range of products not only increased their purchasing power but expanded their ability to accumulate savings and to safeguard their social standing. Together with the repeal of stamp duty on newspapers and advertisements, the reduction or abolition of duties on sugar, tea, coffee, soap, currants, wines, paper and a host of other imported consumables considerably increased the purchasing power of these 'middling sorts' without undermining their own economic security.

Shopkeepers, especially grocers, stood to gain most from the diversification of the market which this process entailed but many voters must also have benefited from it. Recognising that the maintenance of lower taxes relied upon keeping expenditure down, electors also supported measures which improved the efficiency or reduced the size of the military or restructured the far from cost-conscious or meritocratic civil service. The State's 'careful housekeeping' and 'sound administration' of finances mirrored their domestic situation where the avoidance of waste was seen not simply as a virtuous act in itself but as an effective marshalling of scarce resources to maximise both spending and saving. Peel had earned the electorate's gratitude, though not its loyal affection, by initiating the process of fiscal reform in the 1840s; Gladstone, his disciple – responsible for completing the process in the 1850s and 1860s – was to be showered with both.

Despite the apparent remoteness of parliamentary politics and the government's lack of direct interference in the economic life of the country, therefore, it was far from the case that politics was irrelevant or perceived by the electorate as nothing more than a partisan, idealistically-charged game. Ministers, especially the Chancellor of the Exchequer, were capable of influencing the material welfare of the population in ways which were clearly understood by every informed member of the public. Voting was an expression not just of ideals, perhaps not even primarily of these, but of positive expectation of action. By stressing the moral and intellectual superiority of his audiences, Gladstone's speeches of the early 1860s (see pp. 43–4) may have flattered their egos but it was his budgets which lined their pockets.

The leaders and the led

The emphasis in this chapter on popular Liberalism in the mid-Victorian period is partly explained by the fact that comparable information on voting behaviour is not available after the Secret Ballot Act of 1872. But it was also in this period that Liberalism was at its most vibrant, that its causes were unimpeachably virtuous, that its enemies were most clearly identifiable. Through it were channelled the frustrations and aspirations of consumers, taxpayers, and individuals who felt they deserved more recognition by, and justice from, government. It offered the prospect of sweeping away a corrupt, political system in which the 'people' had been treated as mere pawns in the hands of an exclusive, aristocratic class. Its strength lay in its representation of what Gladstone called 'the great social forces' of the age, those classes whose numerical and economic significance had been expanded in the process of Britain's industrial development and whose representatives made up the largest groups in the parliamentary electorate.

The infantry in this crusading army consistently proved themselves more militant than their parliamentary generals, urging them to carry the battle forward with more urgency. The latter, however, were divided in their counsels and preferred to edge their way forward slowly, conscious of the fragile bonds which bound them together. As a loose confederation of individuals they were united more by their opposition to the Tory enemy than by an agreed set of unambiguous 'Liberal' principles and policies. By harnessing the enthusiasm of the troops, however, it was possible for one of these men to lay claim to undisputed leadership, allowing him to impose his own strategy on his far-from-united colleagues. Gladstone, a deserter from the Tory camp, sitting on the sidelines in the 1850s, seemed an unlikely candidate for this role. By the early 1860s, however, he had established a position which remained undisputed for three decades. How he achieved this and what effect it had on the party remain to be explored.

3
Gladstone and the Liberals, 1859–74

The reluctant Liberal

The 1850s were not happy years for Gladstone. Despite holding office as Chancellor of the Exchequer between 1852 and 1855 and gaining a reputation for financial management, he was, like most Peelites, uncertain of his future. He would be happier, he explained to Sir James Graham in 1852, 'on the liberal side of the conservative party, rather than on the conservative side of the liberal party'. As the Tories moved away from die-hard opposition to freer trade after 1846, there seemed to be nothing to prevent him from rejoining his old Tory colleagues. Gladstone frequently found himself following them through the voting lobby, even supporting Derby's doomed minority Tory government in the crucial vote of confidence on 11 June 1859, *after* the alleged formation of the Liberal Party the previous week. He had, he admitted to his Peelite colleagues, Graham and Aberdeen, in May 1858, 'no broad differences of principle from the party opposite'. The Tory leadership, for their part, continued to tempt him with promises of office in their minority governments of 1852 and 1858–9. Even Disraeli wrote to him extolling his 'shining qualities' and offered to stand down as Leader of the House of Commons in 1858. 'I almost went on my knees to him', he recalled later.

However, despite emotional attachment to his old party and many shared assumptions, the reunion did not materialise. Not all the Tories were as keen to welcome him back as Derby was. They distrusted Gladstone's new-found enthusiasm for religious liberty after Maynooth, suspecting that it stemmed from a sympathy with Rome. His spells in office, under Aberdeen and Palmerston, confirmed the impression they had of him as an irredeemable traitor. Gladstone, for his part, had good reason to resist the invitations. Disraeli's prominence in their ranks was a major obstacle. Although Gladstone was often to deny it, and could later be found sympathising with Disraeli, the 'poor fellow', during his wife's illness in 1866, he admitted privately to 'a strong sentiment of revulsion from Disraeli personally'. The fact that Derby acknowledged that many Tories were 'greatly afraid of military reductions' was also a positive disincentive to rejoin them. Gladstone realised that he had little prospect of changing their views unless he took a significant number of ex-Peelites with him. 'There would have been no power', he recalled later, 'unless in company, to give Conservatism a liberal bias in conformity with the traditions of Peel.' Even more fundamental, however, was the view urged upon him in a remarkable letter from Bright in February 1858: 'If you join Lord Derby, you link your fortunes with a constant minority which is every day lessening in numbers and in power. . . . Will you unite yourself with what must be, from the beginning, an inevitable failure?' But Gladstone needed no persuading; if he was to achieve anything in politics he had to possess power and the Tories seemed to offer little prospect of that in the foreseeable future.

Divorced from the Tories, however, Gladstone found it difficult to throw in his lot with the unstable Whig coalitions, largely because he distrusted Palmerston and disagreed fundamentally with much of his foreign policy and enthusiasm for military expenditure. This left him, as he put it, as 'the one remaining Ishmael* in the House of Commons', isolated from all the factions which were vying for office. Although he kept himself in the public limelight by making impassioned parliamentary speeches and supplying the press with information about his movements and intentions, and although he gained by emerging later untainted by association with any of these

* A biblical reference to Abraham's son, cast out of his father's household; a social outcast

personal factions, Gladstone found this a frustrating period of his career. Ambition alone seems to have sustained him and it was this which finally pushed him into clutching gratefully at Palmerston's offer of a post in his new administration in 1859. Whatever his merits as an executive politician, however, he did not seem at that stage to be the future leader of the Liberals and he had no contact with, or conception of, the nature of popular Liberalism in the country.

Wooing the Liberals

It is not clear when Gladstone first appreciated that he had a realistic chance of becoming the Liberals' leader. As early as 1853 he had pondered on the possibility, and various well-wishers had encouraged him in his years out of office, including Bright, who assured him in 1858 that he knew of 'nothing that can prevent your being prime minister'. By the early 1860s there was widespread speculation in the press and at Westminster about his intentions but Gladstone continued to deny that he was actively seeking higher office. 'It is my fixed determination never to take any step whatever to raise myself to a higher level in official life', he explained to the Bishop of Oxford in a letter as late as July 1865. But his reasoning was more ambiguous. 'First because of my total ignorance of my capacity, bodily or mentally to hold such a higher level, and secondly . . . because I am certain that the fact of my seeking it would seal my doom in taking it.' His succession had to look natural, not forced.

To some extent, leadership of the parliamentary party fell naturally into Gladstone's lap. With Palmerston and Russell both advanced in years, a power vacuum was emerging. There was, as W. E. Forster noted in 1864, 'a great prize of power and influence to be aimed at'. Whoever was successful would either have to have the backing of all the sections within the party or be in a position to impose himself upon them. There seemed to be few contenders. Twelve senior members of the cabinet died in the five years after 1859, among them able and popular men like Cornewall Lewis and Sidney Herbert who would have posed a major challenge to Gladstone's succession. 'There were', continued Forster, brusquely, 'no new whigs' who possessed the panache of the 'two terrible old men'. Despite their popularity with the public and the Radical wing, Cobden and Bright were unacceptable to the bulk of the party. They lacked both connections and sufficient administrative experience. 'The want of the Liberal party of a new man was great and felt to be great', concluded Forster. The party, Bright remarked, was in danger of 'going to the dogs', drifting aimlessly.

Few, however, even amongst those who forecast Gladstone's succession, welcomed the prospect of him as leader. He was tolerated in parliament for his administrative talent, but he was hardly admired or liked. He brooked no disagreement and seemed incapable of seeing others' points of view. He did not consult cabinet colleagues before making speeches on matters which were not his direct responsibility. He took no pains to cultivate friendships among the backbenchers, spurning advice from Acland to follow Palmerston's example and make 'easy contact with the small fry' in the parliamentary tea-rooms. His self-righteousness and priggishness offended those who considered themselves more worldly. Palmerston regarded him as 'a dangerous man' only 'partially muzzled' by his need to retain the support of the far from Radical electorate in his Oxford constituency. The Whigs despised his origins and despaired of his rigid economy. Radicals admired his economy but despaired of his views on the American Civil War and his High Anglicanism. He had no foot in any of the rival parliamentary camps, no coterie of admiring supporters to advance his claims.

Gladstone's claims to leadership, therefore, relied not on his hold over parliament, but on a combination of his administrative record and his popularity in the country amongst rank-and-file Liberals and leaders of the organised pressure groups. Although there was an element of luck in the way this came about, it was not an accidental development; nor was it simply a case of the public's adoption of Gladstone as their hero. They were as much 'William's People' as he was 'the People's William'. It was, in many respects, an unlikely partnership, with both sides cherishing a false image of the other's qualities and ambitions, based on imperfect knowledge and understanding. This was not surprising since each side deliberately courted the other, presenting itself adroitly to best effect. The emergence and perpetuation of this unique, awesomely powerful, relationship over three decades remains one of the most striking examples of the power of public opinion. Only recently have historians come to challenge the myths to which it gave rise.

Gladstone's position as Chancellor of the Exchequer was a vital

41

factor in this rise to power. It was not simply that his talents impressed his parliamentary colleagues; they were of immediate material significance to the taxpaying electorate. Not surprisingly, the origins of his popular acclaim can be found in the resumption of his quest for 'economy' and free trade in 1860. The commercial treaty with France, which he and Cobden negotiated that year, and the sweeping reductions in tariffs and duties in the budgets of 1860 and 1861 did much to improve Gladstone's reputation with the free-trade Radicals in the party and consumers in the country. The burgeoning national and provincial popular press joined with them to support his fight to abolish the paper duties – those long criticised, unjustifiable 'Taxes on Knowledge'. This struggle also led to an unexpected constitutional drama in which Gladstone was suddenly cast as the champion of civil liberties against an unrepresentative and class-ridden aristocracy. Departing from convention, the Lords, with Palmerston's overt approval, declined to sanction the abolition of paper duties in 1860, usurping the traditional right of the lower chamber to decide on financial matters. 'I, for one', declared Gladstone, 'am not willing that the House of Commons should hold on sufferance in the nineteenth century what it won in the seventeenth and confirmed and enlarged in the eighteenth century'. Both Bright and the overwhelmingly Liberal popular press rallied behind him as the only member of the front bench who seemed capable of furthering their causes. By the time the offending repeal had been pushed through parliament in the subsequent year's budget, by including it in a general finance bill which the Lords were unwilling to veto, Gladstone's standing among Radicals and in the country had markedly increased. His carefully qualified declaration in favour of the ultimate extension of the franchise in 1864 and the defeat of the Liberals' parliamentary reform bill at the hands of the Tories and a small band of Liberal defectors, christened the Adullamites★ by John Bright, further inflated Gladstone's reputation as a reformer. Reactionary forces seemed to be holding back his reforming impulses. Despite Gladstone's initial support for the Confederate cause in the American Civil War, therefore, the Radicals, including the influential Bright, gave him their public support. Apparently without

★1 Samuel, 22, v. 2: a reference to the cave Adullam where 'everyone that was discontented' gathered around King David

seeking it, simply by pursuing his crusade for cheap government, Gladstone had become a popular figure.

As a result of his repeal of the paper duties, Gladstone could generally rely on a favourable press, the most powerful and rapidly expanding public medium of the day. Largely Liberal by inclination but particularly grateful to Gladstone for his part in reducing the costs of production, the new press lavished fulsome praise upon him, in marked contrast to *The Times* whose earlier virtual monopoly on news had now been broken. The *Daily Telegraph* which had symbolically absorbed the old Peelite journal, the *Morning Chronicle*, was unstinting in its praise. This was not totally fortuitous. Realising the potential of the press, Gladstone had long deliberately courted it. Even in the 1850s he regularly supplied journalists with details of his activities; from about 1860 he went further. Not only did he supply them with details of his movements and opinions, in modern parlance, he 'leaked' official information anonymously to his contact at the *Telegraph*, Thornton Leigh Hunt. The press was to prove a valuable ally over the subsequent decades. Even after the national newspapers began to desert the Liberal camp in the late 1870s, those in the provinces, which reached a wider audience, continued to be loyal to the party. Gladstone had not only helped create a powerful new propaganda agency, he benefited directly from it in the process.

The press was particularly useful in broadening the impact of another of Gladstone's initiatives – public speaking. Audiences who had strained to hear the great man in halls not designed for their acoustic qualities, even those who had only stood and watched him drive majestically by, could read in the comfort of their own homes the following day what they had failed to comprehend or even hear. When, in October 1862, Gladstone embarked on his first orchestrated public-speaking tour of the North, the spectacle of him sailing down the Tyne at the head of a convoy of steamers amidst the 'roar of guns and the banks lined or dotted above and below with multitudes of people' was shared by readers all over the country. Gladstone was not alone in recognising the publicity value of such occasions, for among leading Liberals Bright in particular had long recognised that a public speech 'was more read and tells more on opinion than a speech in a debate in the House'. Palmerston had briefly tried his hand at public speaking, although only after taking meticulous precautions to ensure amenable audiences, and without

43

relish or obvious success. After 1862, however, Gladstone became the first prominent politician to engage in it systematically. The venues (nearly all in the north of England), subjects and times were all carefully chosen. As spectacles, Gladstone's appearances were meticulously planned and stage-managed, and they proved ideal vehicles for his theatrical oratory. In his early speeches he promised little that was new, concentrating heavily on the fiscal achievements of the previous decades, but by the second half of the 1860s he was announcing policy at such meetings. His decision to disestablish the Irish Church, for example, was publicly announced unexpectedly to an audience at Southport. He found it all intoxicating and clearly revelled in public adulation, while his wife was ecstatic. 'Oh, I shall never forget that day!' she recalled of his visit to Newcastle. 'It was the first time, you know, that *he* was received as he deserved to be.'

The 1860s also witnessed the emergence of Gladstone as the unlikely champion of several of the diverse causes which had attached themselves to the parliamentary party in the hope of obtaining legislation favourable to their interests. By publicly congratulating Lancashire textile operatives for what he perceived to be their commendable restraint and patience during the Cotton Famine of the early 1860s, he gave the impression that he was sympathetic to the cause of labour. Trade unions' representatives soliciting amendments to bills dealing with the Post Office Savings Banks and Government Annuities bills in 1863 and 1864 to allow them to invest their funds, were cordially received and similarly praised. By 1867 he was stoutly defending the 'Junta', the core of moderate Liberal trade union leaders under the carpenters' leader, Robert Applegarth, who sought to project a respectable image of the labour movement to gain political and legal concessions. Through these contacts, Gladstone came to hold an idealised concept of an upstanding, moral and respectable working class which sustained him until he was disillusioned by what he saw as the rise of 'selfish' labour interests in the 1880s.

He also drew closer to the Nonconformists with whom he also had had no previous formal contact. Baulked in their attempts to obtain satisfactory legislation and lacking influential parliamentary spokesmen – Miall, leader of the Liberation Society had been defeated in the elections of 1857 and 1859 – leading Dissenters turned to Gladstone for assistance. Christopher Newman Hall, a moderate

Congregationalist minister, invited him, as the future leader of 'wise and safe liberalism', to meet selected representatives of what he called this 'large and not uninfluential section of the Liberal party' at a series of meetings in his home from January 1864 onwards. Gladstone had already signalled his willingness to support Nonconformist causes by voting in favour of a bill in 1863 which allowed Dissenting ministers to carry out burial services in Anglican cemeteries. In 1866 he supported the abolition of church rates, long a bone of contention, and he even introduced his own successful measure two years later. He let it be known in 1865 that he would seriously consider disestablishing the Irish Church when 'the practical politics of the day' allowed. Although he also insisted that this move was still a 'remote' possibility, privately he admitted to a shorter time span. 'Heaven knows, perhaps it will be five years, perhaps it will be ten.' In fact it was just two. By 1867 he was openly championing the cause, consolidating his support not just with English Nonconformists but with the Catholic Church which Derby had correctly forecast would be 'bribed' by the Liberals in the 1868 election.

Despite the distrust of him within the parliamentary party, therefore, there was no challenge to Gladstone's assumption of leadership when the aged Russell finally resigned in 1867. His position by then was unassailable. He alone seemed to hold out the prospect of achieving legislative action related to a wide range of grievances and aspirations. Moreover, he enjoyed the support of the Liberal rank and file. Yet the parliamentary Liberals were no nearer solving the problems of sectionalism and poor organisation which had dogged them in the past, and the hopes which the rank and file placed in Gladstone were wildly optimistic. The reality simply did not match his reputation. Despite his association with franchise reform, he was no democrat. Qualifications in his famous speech of 1864 when he announced that 'every sane and not disqualified man has a moral right to vote' made clear that he was not in favour of 'sudden, or violent, or excessive, or intoxicating change' and wished to go no further than an earlier measure which Russell had proposed in 1859. It was Russell and not Gladstone who wished to push on with legislation after Palmerston's death in 1865. It was Bright and not Gladstone who addressed the thronging crowds during the Reform bill crisis of 1866–7. Gladstone declined to address the crowds which

45

gathered in Hyde Park in July 1866 after the defeat of Russell's bill to demand immediate action; neither the occasion nor the subject suited him. Nor was he an unequivocal champion of the rights of labour. In his view there were no irreconcilable differences between masters and men and his ideal workers were essentially deferential ones, displaying the qualities which he praised the Lancashire factory operatives for during the Cotton Famine: 'self command, self control, respect for order, patience under suffering, confidence in the law' and, significantly, 'regard for superiors'. Nonconformists and Catholics were equally deluded if they thought that he fully supported their causes. The abolition of church rates was not the first step towards dismantling the Anglican establishment; it was designed to strengthen it by removing justified grievances against it. Disestablishment of the Anglican Church in Ireland did not herald the withdrawal of the English from that island; it was to persuade Catholics there to accept foreign rule, preferably under a Liberal government. Moulded by his meetings at Newman Hall's, where non-militant representatives had portrayed Nonconformist demands as limited and moderate, he had little conception of the depth of feeling which inspired their militant pressure groups. With his beliefs in individual liberty, the free market and the capacity of reason to change behaviour, he could have no truck with the moral authoritarians in the United Kingdom Alliance. 'How could I,' he asked of the Duchess of Sutherland, 'who drink good wine and bitter beer every day of my life in a comfortable room and among friends, coolly stand up and advise hard-working fellow creatures to take "the pledge"?' In the heady days of courtship, however, neither side recognised, or possibly could afford to acknowledge, the yawning gap which separated them. Marriage was to bring such differences to the fore. It was also to demonstrate the difficulty of divorce.

Leader and Prime Minister, 1867–74

Given the problems which it faced, what is remarkable about Gladstone's first ministry of 1868–74 is not that it ultimately fell into disarray, but that it functioned successfully for so long. The fundamental nature of the demands of the various sections within the party meant that none of them was likely to be completely satisfied with the compromises which government ministers felt it necessary to construct to retain broad-based support. Assessments of Gladstone's role during these difficult years must not lose sight of this continuing susceptibility to sectionalism and the undeniable fact that the problems which the party experienced with him as leader were nothing to those which it would have faced without him, especially as the Tories' political challenge resurfaced after 1868. His leadership strategy in such circumstances revolved around two central requirements: the delivery of just enough in the way of legislative action and political rewards to stave off outright revolt by any section, and the espousal of causes under whose banner all could enthusiastically unite to bully into submission a hostile, Tory-dominated House of Lords and to appeal confidently to the electorate for continued support.

Apart from broad agreement on the need for continuing retrenchment, there was no Liberal legislative programme in the election of 1868, and the drawing up of one would only have served to turn the party in on itself. Irish disestablishment, however, as Gladstone astutely recognised, was a cause behind which secular Radicals, Irish Catholics and Protestant Nonconformists could all unite. 'Whatever Gladstone's task in Ireland would eventually come to comprise', remarks Michael Bentley of the commitment of December 1867, 'his mission was to pacify the Liberal party'. Furthermore, disestablishment would cut the ground from under the Tories, who had also recognised the political capital to be made out of wooing the Irish Catholic voters, promising them concurrent endowment of their own church without dismantling the Irish Anglican establishment. The time, therefore, in Gladstone's parlance, was 'ripe', not because the situation in Ireland was becoming any more unstable, but because it was politically advantageous. Disestablishment was a coup of which Gladstone was justifiably proud. This single issue, and a judicious, balanced representation of the various sectional interests at cabinet level, however, were never going to be enough to sustain party unity for the duration of the administration. Indeed, Irish questions, which were to remain Gladstone's personal obsession, were increasingly contentious and were ultimately the occasion of the government's downfall.

In other areas of policy the initiative for, and details of, bills were, as always, primarily the responsibility of ministers; it was to them, individually and collectively, that the task of balancing competing

47

vested interests fell. Gladstone exercised little influence on, and claimed little credit for, most of his administration's legislative measures. His views on education were largely overridden and he left to Forster the detailed drafting of the Education Act of 1870 which established locally-elected school boards to set up rate-supported schools to 'fill the gaps' in voluntary provision. He was positively unhappy with the contentious Licensing Act of 1872, rejecting even the mild restrictions on the drink trade in it. 'I cannot get him to really interest himself in the subject', moaned Bruce, the Home Secretary. 'Free trade' in the sale of liquor was all Gladstone was interested in and that, Bruce declared categorically, 'the House won't have'. Support for the labour legislation in 1871 was both late and lukewarm. His ambition to effect a complete overhaul of military bureaucracy was frustrated; Cardwell's 1871 initiative to abolish the purchase of commissions was a poor substitute. He was decidedly unhappy about the abolition of university religious tests the same year and the secret ballot of 1872 was something which he accepted only with 'lingering reluctance'.

The legislation that emerged, therefore, was not 'his' and it invariably represented a compromise. As such it disappointed many in the party and its constituent pressure groups. Their hopes unduly raised, the uncompromising militants were distinctly frustrated, while moderate Whigs and backbenchers felt they were being swept along rather more quickly than they really desired. Nonconformists, especially those in the National Education League and Liberation Society, were infuriated by the Education Act because it did not dismantle Anglican schools and even allowed payment of church schools' fees through the rates. Temperance reformers' demands for total prohibition were just as impractical as Gladstone's free-trade aspirations and they were not satisfied with the repeal in 1869 of the Beer House Act of 1830 (which had allowed the sale of beer without the need to obtain a licence from the magistrates) or the imposition of tighter controls on the licensing of public houses in the 1872 Act. The Irish, their expectations raised by the ease with which disestablishment had been achieved, found the Land Act of 1870, which sought to give them security of tenure by legalising customary practices, inappropriate and unworkable; Liberal landowners, however, were already expressing disquiet at the infringements on their rights which such legislative intervention implied. Far from appeasing the

48

Irish, Gladstone's solution merely raised expectations still further, undermining fragile Liberal support there, increasing the appeal of nationalist campaigners. The government's resort to coercion and the detention of nationalist Fenians in 1870 undid much of the good the conciliatory approach may have done elsewhere. Labour leaders, initially satisfied with the Trade Union Act of 1871, which recognised their legal existence by securing their funds if they registered with the Registrar of Friendly Societies, and the Criminal Law Amendment Act of the same year, which sought to clear up outstanding aspects of criminal law affecting them, were soon disenchanted when the judiciary interpreted the latter in such a way as to imply that strike action was illegal.

The government's record on other fronts was equally patchy. Meritocratic and economical Radicals welcomed the extension of competitive examinations in the Civil Service, Cardwell's abolition of purchase in the army and the admission of Dissenters as fellows of the ancient universities. The individualism promised by the 1834 Poor Law Amendment Act's attempted abolition of outdoor relief to able-bodied paupers was also vigorously pursued by the new Local Government Board after 1871. Enthusiasm was tempered, however, by the partial nature of the reforms, particularly the failure to effect a major bureaucratic overhaul of the War Office and Admiralty. Increasingly ominous, too, were vociferous protests from ratepayers about the level of local taxation and the demands which accompanied them for increasing financial relief from the Exchequer. There was little to please either those who yearned for evidence of Britain's overseas might, so eloquently expressed under Palmerston, or those who wished to see an increased commitment to world peace and internationalism. The government was shown to be totally powerless during the crisis which engulfed Europe when Prussia crushed France in 1870; it was seemingly humiliated by the agreement to pay compensation to the United States for damage done by the British privateer, the *Alabama*, during the American Civil War, and by Russia's abrogation in 1870 of the restrictive Black Sea clauses imposed upon her in 1856 after her decisive trouncing in the Crimean War. Far from being able to withdraw from unwelcome and expensive foreign commitments, Gladstone's government found itself reluctantly drawn into colonial struggles in the Gold Coast and Fiji; on the other hand, it was shown to be powerless to stop colonies, beginning with New Zealand in 1870, imposing their own tariffs on British goods.

Time was on the Tories' side. All Disraeli had to do in these circumstances was wait for what Morley called the 'essentially composite character' of the party to reveal itself in 'awkward fissures'. This it finally did over Gladstone's own initiative to reform the Irish universities in 1873. By making the issue a vote of confidence in himself and his government, he was virtually obliged to resign on defeat. His ranks in disarray and his patience finally exhausted, Gladstone duly tendered his resignation to the Queen in March. Despite his earlier indications that, in Lord Aberdare's words, he was 'vexed at the ingratitude of men for whom he has done such great things which would have been simply impossible without him', there is no convincing evidence to suggest that he would have resigned from the leadership then, had a Tory administration been formed, or even in January 1874 had the Liberals been returned triumphant in the general election. As it was, he was given no option but to continue, since the Tories, breaking with tradition, astutely declined the royal invitation to form a minority government. They realised that this would provide a focus for Liberal reunion but that, left in power, their opponents' embarrassing public disagreements would continue to damn them.

Gladstone's solution to the impasse was to return to the tactic which had served him well in 1868. What he was looking for, he explained in a letter to Bright in August, was 'a *positive* force to carry us onwards as a body', one which appealed to the 'average opinion of the party. I do not see that this can be got out of local taxation, or out of the suffrage . . . or out of education. It may possibly, I think, be had out of finance.' Dismissing Robert Lowe from the Chancellorship of the Exchequer, he resumed that office himself and by January 1874 had settled on 'something large and strong and telling' which he thought would benefit the country and, just as importantly, 'lift the party in the public view and estimation'. He would honour pledges he had initially made in 1853 and repeated in the early 1860s to abolish income tax. The Tories would have found abolition a difficult card to counter had Gladstone actually been able to effect it. But to offset some of the revenue which would be lost he had to achieve substantial cuts in military expenditure. The War Office and Admiralty resisted these fiercely and in the snap election called in

January 1874 the mere promise as opposed to the fact of abolition proved insufficient to return the Liberals.

Why the Liberals suffered such a crushing electoral defeat in 1874 has never been adequately explained. There are as many views as there are historians: Disraeli's inspired leadership of the Tories, their superior party organisation, the wholesale disaffection of the influential drink trade, Nonconformist defections and abstentions, English disapproval of the Liberals' association with the Catholic Irish cause, the labour movement's disappointment with the government's failure to unravel the 1871 débâcle – all doubtless contributed to a greater or lesser degree. In Ireland itself, despite the return of nominally Liberal candidates, it was Home Rule which now dictated the political agenda, confirmation of Gladstone's failure to secure that country for his party. The Liberals had offended too many important interests and as Lord Halifax ruefully pointed out, 'The feelings of those who suffer from the removal of abuses are always stronger than those of the general public who are benefited'. It would be unfair to blame Gladstone personally for the defeat. His handling of situations may, on occasions, have highlighted divisions in the party but it did not create them. Apart from constantly endeavouring to explain the art of the possible to immovable fanatics, it is difficult to see what else he could have done during these years. Any attempts to meet in full the demands of one section of the party would have alienated others and would probably have been rejected by a Tory-dominated House of Lords. The full implementation of the UK Alliance's proposals, on licensing, for example, would have seriously jeopardised public support.

Liberal schisms, however, were not new, and they had not prevented the party romping home in every election, except in 1841, since the Reform bill crisis over half a century earlier. The problems in 1874 were more fundamental. They reflected a Liberal failing to come to terms with the priorities and management of the new mass electorate which was no longer numerically dominated by their loyal retail and craft sectors. Not only was their organisation outdated; their issues were increasingly seen as irrelevant. The abolition of income tax would undoubtedly have been a popular cause in the 1860s but Gladstone's dream of a taxpaying franchise had been shattered by 1867 (see p. 11) and with it the overwhelming appeal that this issue had; only a small minority of the expanded electorate paid the tax. His own success in creating the financial settlement in the 1860s now worked against him; fiscal matters no longer aroused the same feelings of indignation. Although historians have consistently emphasised the importance of the middle-class vote (never wholly Liberal above shopkeeper-level anyway, as pollbooks consistently show) Gladstone was acutely aware of the importance of appealing to the new working-class voters, 'the operative class', who, he subsequently observed, 'have determined the elections'. Here, however, he was hard pressed to find an issue other than 'the free breakfast table' – further small reductions in duties. The Tories, keeping their heads down and offering no hostage to fortune by espousing specific policies, presented to Gladstone no opportunity to rally his troops against a common enemy. His own personal popularity had also temporarily ebbed. During his premiership he had not courted mass affection to the same extent as he had done in the 1860s and this had helped Disraeli to stake a rival claim as a public orator. The Tories had also recognised more clearly that the needs of mass electioneering demanded a new form of party organisation with full-time constituency agents, paid for out of party funds, with armies of volunteers and a semblance of public participation in party affairs, in their case, through the new National Union of Conservative and Constitutional Associations.

Gladstone, who was dispirited, even angered by defeat and unattracted by the prospect of prominence and responsibility without power on the fractured opposition front benches, resigned his leadership within two days of the result being known but was persuaded to stay on into 1875 to avoid precipitating an internal crisis. He then retreated to Hawarden to immerse himself in intellectual pursuits and 'axework', leaving the Liberals to heal their rifts or realise that they could not succeed without him. He could not, he insisted, 'give any material aid in the adjustment of difficulties'. Having found it difficult to live with him, the Liberals now found it difficult to live without him. Reluctantly, Hartington took up the reins of leadership, but the front benches, in Bright's opinion, remained 'full of discord' and 'full of jealousy'. Gladstone's determination to retire, however, was, despite his public protestations, a qualified one. He would return to the fray, he announced, if required for 'arresting some great evil or pursuing for the nation some great good'.

It did not take long for a 'great evil' to emerge in the form of Disraeli's handling of the Middle Eastern crisis, and general 'unsound' financial administration. By the summer of 1876 Gladstone was back in harness, his ambition and drive undiminished. After writing *The Bulgarian Horrors and the Question of the East* in just four days, he embarked on lecture tours expounding his views on the Tories' mishandling of the affair. By late 1879, having agreed to vacate the seat in Greenwich which he had first won in 1865 but maintained with a reduced majority in 1874, he was in Scotland, staking his claim to sit for the Tory-dominated seat of Midlothian with well-orchestrated addresses to mass audiences which set new standards of political campaigning and attracted unprecedented national press coverage. His main theme was the iniquities of 'Beaconsfieldism' as he chose to call the Tory administration after Disraeli's elevation to the peerage and assumption of that title, especially its mishandling of foreign affairs and poor financial record. The Liberals' rather unexpected landslide victory in the election of 1880 probably owed more to the poor state of trade, agricultural depression and, possibly, improved party organisation than to the 'Midlothian Campaign'. What this did mean, however, was that it was impossible for either Hartington in the Commons or Earl Granville in the Lords to considering forming a government with Gladstone on the backbenches or even as a subordinate colleague. Reluctantly Victoria was obliged to ask him to form the next government.

4
Doubts, desertions and decline: 1880–94

The old order changes

Superficially the electoral victory of 1880 implied that the old Liberal order which Gladstone understood, accepted and wished to consolidate had survived intact. The rallying cries of sound finance and a responsible approach to foreign affairs reflected a continuation of mid-Victorian policies. In reality, however, the foundations of Liberal hegemony were gradually being undermined as assumptions about human motivation and the role of government were questioned in the wake of fundamental changes in British society. From this time on, the Liberals were to find themselves increasingly out of touch with the forces moulding popular electoral opinion and progressively unsure of their future role, even of their survival. Within half a century they had been virtually eclipsed as a political force by the rise of the Labour Party.

The last quarter of the nineteenth century was to see a considerable diminution in the wealth and power of the landed class which both Gladstone and Disraeli in their different ways had endeavoured to preserve. The dramatic fall in agricultural prices, rents and land values which resulted from influxes of foreign corn in the 1870s and meat and dairy produce during the following decade undermined the economic base on which the landed class's power rested, leading to their gradual withdrawal from politics. After the extension of the suffrage to rural householders in 1884 and the Redistribution Act of 1885 which swept away old county seats replacing them with one-member seats, landed representation in the House of Commons fell significantly while ownership of land gradually ceased to be a prerequisite for elevation to the peerage. Rural unrest, especially in Ireland and the Scottish Highlands, also led to the passing of the Irish Land Act of 1881 and the Crofters' Act five years later which, by guaranteeing 'fair rents' and security of tenure for farmers, challenged previous beliefs about the inviolability of property rights. Even English landowners found their freedom to use their land as they wished restricted by the Ground Game Act of 1880 and the Agricultural Holdings Act of 1883.

The previously undisputed virtues of free trade and minimal government as the keys to future prosperity were also coming under scrutiny. As foreign competition posed a mounting threat to British overseas trade, business interests were to be heard after 1881 calling for 'Fair Trade' and for more government support in securing new markets, possibly by colonial annexations. Spurred on by widely reported expositions of appalling social conditions in London's East End after 1884, other voices demanded a reassessment of the official attachment to the doctrines of unfettered individualism as the most appropriate way of alleviating the problems of poverty, disease, old age and ignorance. Poverty *per se*, they argued, was neither the crime nor the moral failing which official poor law policies assumed; the crime lay in not doing more to remove its causes. It was not enough for government merely to remove civil and political obstacles and assume individuals would be able to fend for themselves; positive assistance was required to combat social disabilities. Partly as a response to this, partly as a response to increased military demands, both the proportion of gross national product absorbed by government and the *per capita* annual cost began to creep up.

On the industrial and commercial front, too, there were changes. In 1851 the world's 'workshop' had been largely that. Few large-scale industrial enterprises existed outside heavy engineering and textiles and, even in the latter, small and medium-sized units predominated. The application of steam power was still in its infancy, and much production, especially of consumer goods, relied on hand technology and artisan organisation. By the last quarter of the

55

century changes were evident in both the nature of production and the social relationships which it engendered. An estimated one million steam horse-power was employed in manufacturing in 1870; by 1907 the figure had risen to over nine million. In trades like shoemaking, factory production rapidly displaced hand technology; in others, like engineering, new tools threatened to 'deskill' the workforce; in yet others, like cotton, the pace of work was gradually increased. Even in retailing, still largely the domain of the small shopkeeper, there were ominous signs of change as co-ops and price-conscious multiples expanded their shares of the market. The heyday of the *petit bourgeois* producer and retailer had passed. A new social order was being created where relations between capital and labour occupied a central role. The days were over when the 'people' or 'productive classes' could be rallied to oppose an irresponsible, unaccountable, parasitic landed class. 'The relations of labour and capital', remarked R. B. Haldane in 1888, 'may prove to be of profound moment as regards the future of Liberalism.'

The pace of change was not rapid, but cumulatively it amounted to a wholesale undermining of the unquestioned foundations on which Gladstone and the Liberals had constructed their view of the world. The moral imperatives and certainties of an order based on individual spiritual and religious beliefs, on the merits of individual self-help and on the efficacy of competitive free trade and minimal government seemed increasingly outdated. Secularism was over-shadowing sectarianism, materialism ousting morality, collective duty overshadowing individual responsibility. Popular expression of these new forces was made possible by further political changes. Whereas the post–1832 franchise had largely reflected the dominance and interests of the small-scale producer and retailer, after the reforms of 1867 and 1884 these groups were swamped by the new working-class electorate. The passage of the Corrupt Practices Act in 1883 merely emphasised what was already patently obvious to many, that the increased numbers of voters demanded new electoral tactics and forms of political organisation. 'Party' support was now to be increasingly important in securing nominations and mobilising voters.

In this new climate, Gladstone's forceful presence and vigorous public campaigns, once so effective because they were so novel, would not be enough to guarantee Liberal victory. The audience and

56

the issues had changed. With the substantial fall in consumer prices and rise in real incomes from the mid-1870s, the urgency of further fiscal reform had passed, displaced by increasing concern over the burden of local rates, a grievance which the Tories with their greater willingness to consider 'doles' (subsidies from the Exchequer) seemed poised to exploit. Mid-Victorian patriotism, based on an assumed superiority which had allowed a liberal treatment of emerging nations, had been replaced by a nationalist xenophobia as overseas challenges emerged. On the other side of the political spectrum new groups like the Social Democratic Federation (1884), Fabians (1884) and Independent Labour Party (1893) were wooing the workers with a very different vision of their rights and duties from that which Gladstone had portrayed in the 1860s – and was still portraying – as the basis of the social order. The 'spectre' of 'Socialism', as it was frequently portrayed in *Punch*, stalked the land, undermining the vertical ties between classes which had been the basis of mid-Victorian Liberal stability. The Liberals needed to find a new role. The problem, in the words of C. P. Scott, editor of the influential *Manchester Guardian*, 'was to find the lines on which the Liberals could be brought to see that the old tradition must be expanded to yield a fuller measure of social justice, a more real equality, an industrial as well as a political liberty'.

Liberals in transition

Neither Gladstone nor his party could avoid the impact of these changes; whether they adjusted successfully to them is another matter.

Michael Bentley's recent analysis of MPs' backgrounds at the time of the 1892 election clearly shows that parliamentary Liberalism had lost much of its landed element. Only 8 per cent could be clearly categorised as coming from a substantial landed background; businessmen and financiers now formed the largest grouping (44 per cent), followed by lawyers (25 per cent) and miscellaneous professionals and journalists (23 per cent). The usual explanation of this transformation is the 'desertion of the Whigs' in 1886 over the issue of Irish Home Rule (see pp. 61–3). This, however, oversimplifies matters. Although those from an 'aristocratic landowning' background were overrepresented in the dissentients, they accounted for

57

only forty-six of the ninety-four (45.7 per cent); the rest, according to Terry Jenkins, were 'industrialists and merchants' (thirty-one or 33 per cent) and lawyers (twenty-one or 22.3 per cent) amounting to a 'significant portion of the Liberal "centre"'. Some Whigs, like the Duke of Argyll, had already resigned over the land reforms in the early 1880s. Other prominent men, like Rosebery, Harcourt, Granville and Kimberley remained loyal. By far the most important factor in the decline of landowning representatives was their deteriorating absolute and relative economic position. Even in the Tory Party, large landowners comprised only 25 per cent of MPs by 1892.

Liberalism's religious connections were also weakened. In Ireland any hopes the party may have had of consolidating the Catholic vote had long since vanished. By the 1880s Nationalism, in the form of Parnell's Irish Parliamentary Party, enjoyed overwhelming support outside Ulster. In the election of 1885 the Liberals failed to win any seats in Ireland. To many on the British mainland, however, the party seemed to be inextricably linked with the Irish Catholic cause. Working-class voters in Lancashire in particular, objected on more materialistic and cultural grounds. The large numbers of Irish immigrants there represented cheap labour and alien values. Nonconformists' ardour for the Liberals' cause also declined, even amongst Dissenting clerics, once their most devoted followers. The grievances of a lawless, popish minority were seemingly being given precedence over their own continuing demands for English disestablishment and temperance reform. But Nonconformity was no longer the power it once had been. Outside Wales, Scotland and Ulster, where it represented more than adherence to specific dogma, it had lost much of its *raison d'être*. No longer discriminated against in any material way, Nonconformity's grievances now seemed irrelevant in an increasingly secular world. As early as 1874 the so-called 'Nonconformist Revolt' had shown that it could substantially influence neither Liberal policy nor the level of mass support for the party. The expansion of the electorate in 1867 and 1884 had swamped more than the loyal shopkeepers and artisans; it had given the vote to the majority of non-churchgoers in the country. The Liberals would have to find a new cause.

Organised labour, in the form of trade unionism, seemed to offer a promising ally. As yet it represented but a small proportion, less than one million, of the adult workforce, but many realised that it held the key to the development of British politics into the next century. The loyalty of the trade union movement did not seem to have been unduly affected by the Liberals' unfortunate Criminal Law Amendment Act of 1871 or by the Tories' subsequent repeal of the offending sections four years later. Its leaders continued to look to the party for the fulfilment of their aims: the return of more working-class MPs and relatively minor government intervention in labour relations, most noticeably over employers' liability. On the whole, they were content that government should lay down the conditions under which they could function effectively as industrial bargaining agents; they did not seek an increase in the State's power. 'Socialism' repelled all but a minority of activists. Working through the TUC's Parliamentary Committee and the Liberal Electoral Committee, union leaders achieved some success; working men sat as 'Lib-Lab' MPs by 1886 and Henry Broadhurst, Secretary of the Stonemasons' Union, became Under-Secretary at the Home Office in that year.

But Liberal enthusiasm for labour's cause was limited. The only signs in the famous Newcastle Programme of October 1891 that the Liberals as a body were willing to come to terms with the growing labour interest were vague expressions of support for legislation on employers' liability and the limitation of hours of work. As trade union membership grew during and after the burst of New Unionism 1889–91 which encompassed less skilled workers, working-class representation failed to increase. Local constituency Liberal parties proved reluctant to nominate working men as parliamentary candidates or JPs. Individuals like Keir Hardie and Ramsey Mac-Donald, who had tried initially to gain Liberal nominations, became increasingly frustrated with the party and sought alternative routes into parliament, first through the Independent Labour Party in 1893 and ultimately, with some trade union backing, through the Labour Representation Committee of 1900, the forerunner of the Labour Party. Professionals and journalists in the Liberal Party might talk about coming to terms with labour's demands, but the serried ranks of businessmen on the parliamentary benches and constituency committees, who dominated the party machinery and finances, proved more difficult to convince.

The Liberals were equally tentative in edging towards new conceptions of their philosophy and new party organisation. Much of the initial impetus for this came from the Radical ex-mayor of Birmingham, Joseph Chamberlain. From the mid-1870s he increasingly championed a more positive view of the State's role in social reform and in 1877 he was a central figure in the establishment of the National Liberal Federation which he hoped would promote his views in the party. Working on the assumption that grass roots opinion was more Radical than that of the parliamentary party, he hoped this body would offer 'direct participation of all members of the party in the direction of policy, and in the selection of those particular measures of reform or of progress to which priority shall be given'. This was to be achieved on a 'representative basis, that is, by popularly elected committees of local associations, and by the union of such local associations, by means of their freely chosen representatives, in a general federation'.

The initiative soon ran into difficulties. Chamberlain's views carried little weight during the Liberal administration of 1880–5 or in the drawing up of the party's programme in the election of 1885. Frustrated and disillusioned, he launched his own Radical 'Unauthorised Programme', calling for the community through the State to 'discharge its responsibilities and its obligations to the poor . . . by which we shall do something to remove the excessive inequality in social life which is now one of the greatest dangers as well as a great injury to the State'. Despite being considerably toned down during the campaign, the programme alarmed many moderates in the party, especially among the Whigs, who remained far from convinced that the future lay in the direction signposted by Chamberlain. Regionalism and sectionalism also dogged the NLF from the start so that in its early years it did little more than mirror the advanced views of Birmingham Radicals, the so-called 'Gas and Water Socialists' who had promoted municipal provision of services in the 1870s. Since London Liberalism had little in the way of local organisation, it remained virtually unrepresented, even after the federation's headquarters had been moved to the capital in 1886. Scotland, too, was largely unaffiliated. Lancashire Liberals saw it for what it was, a vehicle for the promotion of Chamberlain's political career, and shunned it. As membership gradually increased, however, so its Radical hue faded. By 1886, when Chamberlain defected from the party over Home Rule (see pp. 61–2), it was already firmly behind Gladstone. Only from the mid-1890s was the reforming impetus renewed as a clique of 'Progressive' Liberals constructed a new vision of a more interventionist state and a new concept of freedom which was to form the basis of the 'New Liberalism' exhibited during Liberal governments after 1906. Yet others, however, the Liberal Imperialists, were seeking to counteract the Tories' monopoly of 'national' interests and to make fuller use of Britain's overseas assets, widely defined, to rejuvenate what appeared to be an increasingly ailing and conflict-ridden country.

These anxieties and uncertainties about the party's future at parliamentary level were also felt by many of the electorate from 1886. Residual loyalty remained among many who could never bring themselves to vote Conservative, but low electoral turnouts before 1906 suggest that they were increasingly likely to abstain, disillusioned with their leaders' performance. 'Even such of them as can be induced at the election to vote for the Liberal candidate', observed Sidney Webb of the London workers in 1888, 'are in the party but not of it. There is an almost universal conviction among them that its aims are not theirs and that its representatives are not those whom they would have chosen.' There was an increasing realisation among Liberal leaders that the party had to harness what Gladstone had once called the 'great social forces' of the age if their party was to survive.

The Gladstonian incubus

Presiding over the increasingly anxious and disoriented party until he resigned in March 1894 at the advanced age of eighty-four was the towering figure of William Ewart Gladstone. Rather than being seen as the potential saviour of his party, however, Gladstone was increasingly viewed as a positive liability.

Nothing reflects this better than Gladstone's hopeless obsession with Ireland. The record of his second administration of 1880–5 was dominated by the Irish Question which Gladstone optimistically assumed had been solved by earlier legislation. In contrast to the late 1860s, however, when Gladstone had taken a conscious decision to introduce reform, the crisis was sparked off by an agricultural depression in Ireland which provoked widespread demands from farmers for immediate legislative action on rents, tenure and the right of tenants to sell unexpired leases to whomever they chose – the

'3Fs' for short: fair rents, fixity of tenure and free sale.* Led by overt nationalists like Charles Stewart Parnell and Michael Davitt, whose Irish Land League orchestrated the agitation, the 'Land War' posed a serious threat to legitimacy of British rule in Ireland. Reluctantly Gladstone's government conceded to the farmers' demands in the Irish Land Act of 1881 and the Arrears Act the following year, only to find that this did little to dampen enthusiasm for the nationalist cause. After the shattering Liberal defeats in Ireland in the election of 1885 Gladstone unilaterally concluded that some form of devolved government short of independence, 'Home Rule', was the only option. A startled world and Liberal Party received the news in December 1885 after his son Herbert had indicated his father's intentions in conversation with journalists.

From then on the Irish Question hung like an albatross round the party's neck. Unable to accept the constitutional implications of the proposals, one third of the parliamentary party deserted the following year, ostensibly forming their own group of Liberal Unionists, but effectively being increasingly drawn into the Conservative camp by the continuing prominence of Home Rule in the Liberal programme. Even where Gladstone's Irish policy did not positively alienate English voters, it failed positively to appeal to them. At worst, Home Rule appeared to be pandering to an obstreperous, racial, religious minority, at best to be simply irrelevant to their own material needs. Gladstone's insistence that it was a morally superior cause rang hollow during the scandals which surrounded Parnell after 1887, culminating in his public disgrace in 1890 when he was cited in the O'Shea divorce case. Not since his early days in politics had Gladstone committed himself to such an impractical and unpopular cause. Even in 1893, when he succeeded in pushing it through the Commons, Home Rule foundered inevitably in the Lords; but this time there was no expression of public outrage at such aristocratic obstinacy, no universal press condemnation of their action as there had been during the early 1860s' controversy over the paper duties. Gladstone's instinct was to call for an immediate dissolution on the issue but his cabinet colleagues, more realistically, objected. 'I received', he remarked, 'a hopelessly adverse reply.' Any

*For the background to this see M. J. Winstanley, *Ireland and the Land Question, 1800–1922* (Lancaster Pamphlet, Methuen, 1984)

semblance of a legislative programme during the Liberal government of 1892–5 was destroyed by the time-consuming, controversial nature of the Irish Question.

The destructive obsession with Ireland was only one of a long catalogue of criticisms levelled at Gladstone's leadership which predated even his commitment to Home Rule. During his second ministry of 1880–5 he had offended colleagues whom he could ill afford to offend. Although Joseph Chamberlain's power base in the party was never as strong as he made out, he, like Gladstone before him, claimed, through the National Liberal Federation, to enjoy significant extra-parliamentary support. Gladstone, however, had to be persuaded to give him a cabinet post in 1880 and was personally offensive during the formation of his third ministry in 1886. Chamberlain's desertion in 1886, many have suggested, was as much out of personal disaffection as principled disagreement over Home Rule since he was subsequently to put forward his own federal scheme of government for Ireland. All this, however, merely confirmed Gladstone's view that he was a self-seeking careerist and, as such, no loss to the party. He made no effort to win him back. Gladstone's treatment of other colleagues in cabinet and in opposition was equally high-handed. Out of office after 1886 and, for the first time, leader of a minority opposition, he exhibited few of the skills which Disraeli had displayed in the early 1870s. He rarely ascertained his colleagues' collective views and persistently refused to form a shadow cabinet. Rather than make attempts to reunite his party, he regarded the desertions of 1886 as a corrective purge, vital if Liberalism was to retain its purity. 'The mismanagement of personal relations', concludes Feuchtwanger in his biography, 'was one indication among many that old age was increasing Gladstone's egotism and loss of touch.'

Gladstone also offered nothing constructive to the emerging debate on the party's future. Returned to office in 1880 he had envisaged little beyond correcting the abuses of 'Beaconsfieldism' and the reintroduction of 'sound finance', and it was with some reluctance that he realised that more was needed. He was, remarked Rosebery ruefully in 1892, echoing a widely felt sentiment, 'not in touch with the new order of things'. He despised what he called the 'constructionism' of his Radical colleagues, Chamberlain and Dilke, when they launched their 'Unauthorised Programme' in 1885. He railed against what he regarded as the 'selfish instincts' behind new appeals to the working-class voter and continued to pray optimistically for a recognition of the moral worthiness of causes. He was 'vexed', he wrote rather despairingly to John Morley in 1892, 'to see portions of the labouring class beginning to be corrupted by the semblance of power, as other classes have been tainted and warped by its reality'. 'Nothing but disappointment awaits the working class', he told a receptive audience at All Souls, Oxford in 1890, 'if they yield to exaggerated anticipations which are held out to them by the Labour Party.' He remained unconvinced of the wisdom of legislation restricting working hours which both the TUC and National Liberal Federation were promoting in the early 1890s. He could not, he insisted, change his ways; he was too old for that. His handling of foreign affairs, especially his failure to relieve the heroic, but wilfully disobedient, General Gordon at Khartoum in 1885, also vividly illustrated both his unhappiness with Britain's expanding imperial role in Africa and the yawning gulf which now separated him from a jingoistic British public. 'GOM', the 'Grand Old Man', was temporarily and cruelly dubbed 'MOG', 'Murderer of Gordon', by his enemies.

By the late 1880s, Gladstone was, as he sometimes admitted, a 'survivor' from a previous age who found it difficult to adapt to the new political climate. Aloof, unconcerned with cultivating a successor, improving party policy and organisation or raising morale, uncompromising, literally and intellectually deaf, lacking any sense of proportion, he was also increasingly viewed as a positive liability by some of his colleagues. 'What we want,' fumed an exasperated James Stansfeld in 1885, 'is that Gladstone should vanish and the people reassert themselves.' Nine years later, when he finally bowed out, his colleagues did not feel apprehension or regret, but relief.

A captainless crew

Why though, did these Liberals, clearly chafing under the autocratic rule of this 'old, wild and incomprehensible man' as Queen Victoria called him in 1892, not ditch him, forcing him to carry through his repeated threat to resign? Indeed, why did some of them positively urge him to stay on?

Part of the answer lies in the continued public fascination with all things 'Gladstonian'. However unwelcome some his policies may have been, by this time he was the centre of a personality cult and adulation of the faithful showed little signs of ebbing. Sales of Gladstone memorabilia – portraits, decorated pottery, souvenir programmes and speeches – reached new heights; even his wife, totally convinced of William's unparalleled gifts and as infatuated with his public as she was with his private face, enjoyed unprecedented attention for a politician's wife, her smiling face beaming out from the centre of gold-rimmed wall plates. The 'royals' were not the only family to symbolise late Victorian domestic values, and Hawarden rivalled regal residences as a place of pilgrimage where the faithful could admire Gladstone's collection of axes and perhaps even watch the great man in action symbolically felling a tree. Gone were Gladstone's self-deluding protestations about not seeking such popularity; both he and his family courted and relished such attention. It was no accident that Gladstone was the first politician to make use of the new technology of audio-recording to preserve his voice for posterity.

His public performances were awesome for the emotion they engendered. 'You can hardly imagine the wild beauty and excitement of one of these galloping drives', wrote Gladstone's daughter Mary after his entry into Edinburgh in November 1879 at the height of the Midlothian campaign, 'the lurid light of the torches and bonfires, the brilliant glare of the electric lights and fireworks, the eager faces and waving hands and shouting voices.' A decade later his appeal was undiminished, his advanced years imparting a mystic, guru-like quality to his carefully stage-managed public performances. On a visit to Liverpool in 1886 he appeared, remarked the Irish nationalist journalist T. P. O'Connor, like a 'miraculous saint among masses of idolators'. However much Gladstone protested that it was his message that mattered, it was his actions that remained imprinted in the memory. Even rationalist supporters like Morley clearly found it intoxicating. 'To think of the campaign without the scene', he wrote, was akin to reading 'a play by candle-light among the ghosts of an empty theatre.' As some historians have pointed out, such personality cults, uncompromising dogmatism, undiminished sense of mission and appeals to moral superiority are more commonly associated with totalitarian regimes of the twentieth century than the pluralist democracy that had evolved in Victorian Britain. Although it was impossible to put a precise electoral value on this, the Liberals were unwilling to jeopardise it by deliberately spurning Gladstone's leadership. Gladstone might have been a dangerous man to have as a friend, but he might be even more dangerous to have as an enemy.

But the roots of Liberal acquiescence went deeper than this. Within the parliamentary party, despite the changing relative importance of various groupings, little had altered since Gladstone had first imposed himself upon it in the early 1860s. As its members were only too well aware, they represented a loose confederation of interests. In the words of an astute Nonconformist commentator, the Revd J. Guinness Rogers, in 1895, the Liberals were 'a conglomerate party' riven with 'opposing cliques and disunited forces'. Deprived of Gladstone's overarching presence all sections of the party feared they would simply drift apart. 'There are some people, I think', remarked Harcourt to Ponsonby, Victoria's secretary, as early as 1882, 'who have not realised how much more uncomfortable things will be for *everybody* when he is gone. After all, he is the linchpin of the coach.' The disaffected Chamberlain was correct both in his surmise of 1888 that 'the Gladstonian period is slowly coming to an end . . . its central idea is doomed' and in his forecast that 'it will leave great confusion behind'. What David Hamer has described as 'the vast uncoordinated and incoherent set of reform proposals' which were passed at the annual conferences of the National Liberal Federation, bore little relation to a coherent party programme and gave no indication of the priority which each policy would be given. 'Where', pleaded Herbert Samuel in the first issue of the *Progressive Review* in 1896, 'is the synthesis, the unity of principle and of policy, which shall give solidarity of structure, singleness of aim, economy of force, consistency of action, to this medley of multifarious effort?'

In the past, when they had been unable to agree, Liberals had often been able to unite in righteous indignation against the actions of a common political enemy. Unfortunately the Tories, in power continuously between 1886 and 1905 apart from the brief, lame Liberal administration of 1892–5, refused to oblige their rivals by adopting a die-hard reactionary stance. Under Salisbury's careful stewardship, they revealed themselves to be remarkably pragmatic, in tune with the new middle-class aspirations of what their leader called 'Villa Toryism', adept at tapping working-class cultural conservatism, and imaginative in their handling of the thorny Irish land question. Confident that they could make further inroads into urban areas, they even willingly abandoned 'county seats' in the Redistribution Act of 1885, in favour of single member constituencies. The introduction of democratically elected county councils in 1888 and free education in 1891 were also notable Tory coups. All this was too much for exasperated Liberals who constantly cried foul, claiming that their policies were being hijacked by their opportunistic opponents. The disconcerting fact was that Liberals no longer had anything distinctive to offer the electorate except outdated causes like disestablishment and temperance reform – which had lost both their relevance and their popular appeal – and, as ever, Ireland. The landslide victory of 1906 did not represent a new dawn for the Liberals, but a temporary eclipse of the Tories who, for once, had committed a tactical blunder by reverting to the protectionism which had caused their collapse over half a century earlier.

By the time Gladstone finally relinquished the reins of power in March 1894, the Liberals still had no clear idea of what their future role would be. The election of the following year emphasised the low state of their fortunes in the country. Their tally of English seats dropped from 189 to a low of 112 out of a possible 456 and even in Wales the margin over their rivals narrowed. The year 1900 proved to be little better, the slightly higher English total of 123 being partially offset by Scottish losses.

It is tempting to blame Gladstone for this impasse. He had so totally dominated the party for thirty years that constructive debate had been largely quashed. After 1886 in particular, his intransigent stand on Home Rule delayed planning for the future. Everything remained in the air. Once the Gladstonian incubus had been lifted, however, the true nature of the Liberal dilemma was revealed for all to see. Without its captain, the potentially mutinous crew drifted aimlessly. Neither Rosebery, who replaced him in 1894, nor Harcourt who succeeded Rosebery in 1896 offered much in the way of positive or charismatic leadership.

Surveying the scene in 1898, the year of Gladstone's death, a despairing Asquith, himself destined to preside over both an apparent Liberal resurgence and the subsequent final disintegration of the party between 1908 and 1916, could find no 'rallying cry for a broken army . . . the effectiveness of the party as a potential instrument is crippled . . . the new birth has not yet come'. Rosebery's nightmare vision of the 'elimination of Liberalism, leaving the two forces of Socialism and Reaction to face each other' seemed only too real. Whether the 'New Liberalism' which eventually emerged in the Liberal governments after 1906 really did represent a fundamental reshaping of political outlook and whether it would have proved enough to stifle Labour's development as a separate political party had not the issues involved in managing the war effort of 1914–18 split the party asunder, is, as they say, another story.

5
Conclusion

Much historical literature on Gladstone has concentrated on understanding how and why he functioned as he did. Such studies have involved trying to generalise from a mountain of surviving detailed evidence, much of it generated by Gladstone himself. So close has been the canvas, so fine the brushwork, that it has often proved difficult to conceive of the broader portrait. The interpretations proffered have often revealed more about the viewers, especially those who sympathised with the great man, than they have about the complexity of Gladstone's character. Despite meticulous recent scholarship, it still remains difficult to assess the precise contribution which the various aspects of Gladstone's complex personality made to his public life: the importance of moral certainties, rooted in religious belief; his unambiguous belief in the values of free trade and individual responsibility; his concern to preserve the established social order; even, perhaps, his undiminished political ambition.

But there are other questions which can be asked of his career. What, one is tempted to speculate, would have been the course of nineteenth-century history had Gladstone never been born? Whatever Gladstone's innermost thoughts may have been, what was their importance to the world in which he lived? Such questions remain impossible to answer satisfactorily, but posing them is, nevertheless, a useful exercise, since it brings into sharper focus a fundamental disagreement about how the past should be interpreted. On the one hand, there are those who tend to subscribe to Thomas Carlyle's famous dictum that 'No great man lives in vain. The history of the world is but the history of great men'. On the other, there are those who stress what Gladstone himself called 'great social forces', relegating the role of the individual to that of an enabler, a catalyst in the process of change.

In this context it is important to appreciate what Gladstone did not do. He did not 'invent' Liberalism. This predated his association with the parliamentary party and owed its origins and its vitality to the forces unleashed by economic and social change in Britain. Deprived of Gladstone's leadership its energies may have been dissipated, but it is inconceivable that its political representatives would not have enjoyed considerable electoral success in the mid-nineteenth century. However significant Gladstone may have seemed at the time, electoral behaviour was largely determined by voters' occupations, religious loyalties, wealth or areas of residence. What Gladstone gave to popular Liberalism was an identifiable public face with which the Liberal electorate could easily associate, and a voice which proclaimed, possibly unintentionally, the widely accepted platitudes of the age. His strength derived from a mutually beneficial, reciprocal relationship which he enjoyed with party supporters in the country. Who influenced whom is a difficult tangle to unravel, but it is clear that neither the Liberal Party, nor the less easily defined creed of 'Liberalism', were ever unequivocally Gladstone's.

We should also be careful not to award Gladstone undue credit for the legislative measures of Liberal administrations. While it remains true that his grasp of financial matters undoubtedly contributed significantly to the smooth implementation of a free-trade policy in the 1850s and 1860s, much of the inspiration for his actions came from his mentor, Peel, and much of the credit he received reflected the widespread support which already existed for such a policy. Later, Gladstone's unassailable position allowed him to impose his own peculiar passions on the party. His decision to concentrate on Irish disestablishment in 1868, for example, was a masterly stroke of political calculation which did much to reunite the Liberals after the divisive blow inflicted on them by the Tories' Reform Act the previous year. Even this, however, needs to be viewed in the light of mounting extra-parliamentary pressure for disestablishment and the Tories' own proposals to deal with the religious question in Ireland. Whether most of the Liberals' other legislative reforms originated from shared ideological values or were necessary, pragmatic responses to perceived needs – an issue which is more usually discussed in historical literature dealing with the growth of government – is immaterial here. In neither interpretation is the 'great statesman' theory awarded more than a supporting role. Apart from Irish issues and fiscal reform, Gladstone had little, if any, direct involvement in, or influence on, the framing of domestic legislation. In all probability, many of the domestic reforms which are associated with his name or his ministries would have reached the statute book without him, in much the same way as those associated with Disraeli's ministry did. Despite protestations about applying moral criteria to foreign affairs, Gladstone found himself acting in much the same way as every other prime minister to preserve British material interests overseas.

Gladstone's leadership of the party was also clearly a mixed blessing. Although his position was never seriously challenged, at no stage of his career was he entirely free of internal criticism. The marriage with the parliamentary Liberals was essentially one of convenience, and it worked because no faction felt confident enough to contemplate divorce until 1886, so great was his personal reputation. Effective leadership, however, demanded more than the ability to sustain personal popularity and it is possible to counterbalance the list of his alleged virtues – strength of purpose, political calculation, grasp of administrative and financial affairs, public oratory – with a catalogue of significant failings. He was stubborn, inflexible, took little note of colleagues' views, imposed his own crusades on the party, took little interest in party organisation and, above all, failed to recognise the need to reassess Liberal values in the last quarter of the century. Instead of meeting the broader domestic challenges which the age presented head-on, Gladstone committed himself and his party to the divisive and unrealistic cause of Home Rule, contributing significantly to the Liberals' unhappy electoral performances after 1886.

Tempting though it is to attribute the Liberals' problems to Gladstone's increasingly outdated style of politics and inflexibility, it is also the case that Liberals themselves were unsure about how to

71

adapt as the social and economic bases of their beliefs crumbled. Just as it is difficult to imagine the Liberals languishing in the political wilderness in the mid-Victorian period without Gladstone, so, too, it is difficult to envisage them enjoying political supremacy in the closing decades of the century without him. Individualism, an emphasis on moral issues, sectarian loyalties, the overriding importance of fiscal policy, even free trade – all these were being seriously questioned in a world where relations between capital and labour at home and the threat of foreign competition overseas increasingly dominated political debate. Whether Gladstone's presence seriously retarded the party's adaptation to the new circumstances, or whether it sustained its popularity longer than would otherwise have been the case is less clear. Only one thing is certain, adaptation there would have to be, and Gladstone's overpowering personality could do nothing to prevent it. He was as much a product of his age as he was an architect of its fortunes.

Appendix

British election results, 1857–1900

		1857	1859	1865	1868	1874	1880	1885	1886	1892	1895	1900
England												
Boroughs	Lib	216	202	198	198	144	202					
	Cons	107	121	126	93	143	85					
Counties	Lib	50	45	48	45	27	54					
	Cons	94	99	99	127	145	118					
Total	Lib	266	247	246	243	171	256	241	123	189	112	123
	Cons	201	220	225	220	288	203	214	332	262	343	332
	Others*							1	1	5†	1	1
Scotland												
	Lib	38	38	41	52	40	53	58	43	50	39	34
	Cons	15	15	12	8	20	7	8	27	20	31	36
	Crofters							4				
Ireland												
	Lib‡	55	48	55	65	70	77	—	—	—	1	1
	Cons	50	57	50	40	33	26	16	17	21	19	19
	Irish Nat							85	84	80	81	81
Wales												
	Lib	14	14	18	22	19	28	30	24	31	25	28
	Cons	15	15	11	8	11	2	4	10	3	9	6

	1857	1859	1865	1868	1874	1880	1885	1886	1892	1895	1900
UK Total											
Lib	373	347	360	382	300	414	330	190	270	177	186
Cons	281	307	298	276	352	238	250	395	315	411	402
Others							90	85	85	82	82

*Irish Nationalist T. P. O'Connor sat for Scotland Division, Liverpool, from 1885
†Includes four Independent Labour Party members
‡Includes 'Home Rulers' in 1874 and 1880
University seats included in boroughs before 1885. Division thereafter

	1885	1886	1892	1895	1900
Lib	1	—	—	—	—
Cons	8	9	9	9	9

Liberal Unionists included in Conservative totals from 1886

Select bibliography

This should not be viewed as a definitive bibliography for either Gladstone or the Victorian Liberal Party. Its intention is to provide additional reading material to support the themes explored in this booklet. Place of publication is London unless otherwise stated.

By far the most accessible of the recent scholarly biographies is H. C. G. Matthew, *Gladstone, 1809–74* (Oxford, 1986, pbk 1988) which is a collection of the author's introductions to *The Gladstone Diaries with Cabinet Minutes and Prime Ministerial Correspondence* (nine volumes, Oxford, 1968–86; the earlier volumes were edited by M. D. R. Foot). Only the first volume of R. T. Shannon's detailed biography has so far appeared; *Gladstone, vol. 1, 1809–65* (1982). Among the earlier biographies, E. J. Feuchtwanger, *Gladstone* (1975), P. Magnus, *Gladstone* (1954) and the less comprehensive study by P. Stansky, *Gladstone* (1979) all still have much to recommend them. Despite its overtly pro-Gladstonian stance, John Morley's classic three-volume biography of 1903, *The Life of William Ewart Gladstone* is still hard to beat as a quarry for material and ideas. A. F. Thompson, 'Gladstone', *History Today* (1952) and D. Hamer, 'Gladstone: the making of a political myth', *Victorian Studies* (1978) are both rather critical pieces in their different ways. There are also two useful collections: B. Kinzer (ed.), *The Gladstonian Turn of Mind* (1985) and P. J. Jagger (ed.), *Gladstone, Politics and Religion* (1985).

There are a number of studies of the importance of religion in Gladstone's political career: P. Butler, *Gladstone: Church, State and Tractarianism* (Oxford, 1982); B. Hilton, 'Gladstone's theological politics' in M. Bentley and J. Stevenson (eds), *High and Low Politics in Modern Britain* (Oxford, 1983); G. I. T. Machin, 'Gladstone and nonconformity in the 1860s', *Historical Journal* (1974); J. P. Parry, 'Religion and the collapse of Gladstone's first government, 1870 –74', *Historical Journal*, (1982); J. P. Parry, *Democracy and Religion: Gladstone and the Liberal Party, 1867–1875* (Cambridge, 1986); A. Ramm, 'Gladstone's religion', *Historical Journal* (1985). R. T. Shannon, *Gladstone and the Bulgarian Agitation* (1963) highlights both the moral side of Gladstone's campaign and the political impact it made.

F. W. Hirst, *Gladstone as Financier and Economist* (1931), although useful, should be treated with caution; it was written as a polemical tract for the times. More balanced assessments of Gladstone's financial management are B. Baysinger and R. Tollison, 'Chaining Leviathan: the case of Gladstonian finance', *History of Political Economy* (1980); A. Hawkins, 'A forgotten crisis: Gladstone and the politics of finance during the 1850s', *Victorian Studies* (1983); H. C. G. Matthew, 'Disraeli, Gladstone and the politics of mid-Victorian budgets', *Historical Journal* (1979).

Views on Gladstone's Irish policy have moved on since J. L. Hammond, *Gladstone and the Irish Nation* (1938). Not all are as damning as J. Vincent, 'Gladstone and Ireland', *Proceedings of the British Academy* (1977) but they are nevertheless critical. Among the shorter, more accessible pieces are E. D. Steele, 'Gladstone and Ireland', *Irish Historical Studies* (1970) and A. Warren, 'Gladstone, land and social reconstruction in Ireland, 1881–87', *Parliamentary History* (1983). W. C. Lubenow, 'Irish Home Rule and the great separation of the Liberal Party in 1886', *Victorian Studies* (1983) is more concerned with the impact on the party.

A. Hawkins, *Parliament, Party and the Art of Politics in Britain, 1855–59* (1987); A. Ramm, 'The parliamentary context of cabinet government, 1868–74', *English Historical Review* (1984) and T. A. Jenkins, *Gladstone, Whiggery and the Liberal Party, 1874–1886* (Oxford, 1988) deal primarily with parliamentary affairs. M.

Barker, *Gladstone and Radicalism, 1885–1894* (Hassocks, 1975), H. V. Emy, *Liberals, Radicals and Social Politics, 1892–1914* (Cambridge, 1973), M. Bentley, *The Climax of Liberal Politics, 1868–1918: British Liberalism in Theory and Practice* (1987) and D. Hamer, *Liberal Politics in the Age of Gladstone and Rosebery* (Oxford, 1972) all contain material on the strains within the party in the closing decades of the century. It is still difficult to beat H. J. Hanham, *Elections and Party Management: politics in the time of Gladstone and Disraeli* (1959) as a survey of the organisation of extra-parliamentary politics. D. Hamer, *The Politics of Electoral Pressure* (Hassocks, 1977) contains much detail on the main pressure groups within the party. D. W. Bebbington, *The Nonconformist Conscience: chapel and politics, 1870–1914* (1982) sheds valuable light on the relationship with Liberalism. There is still remarkably little on the nature of the Liberal electorate apart from J. Vincent's pioneering works, *The Formation of the British Liberal Party, 1857–68* (1966, pbk, 1972) and *Pollbooks: How Victorians Voted* (Cambridge, 1967) and T. J. Nossiter's valuable *Influence, Opinion and Political Idioms in Reformed England* (Hassocks, 1975). Recent case studies include T. A. Mcdonald, 'Religion and voting in an English borough: Poole in 1859', *Southern History* (1983) and A. Phillip, 'Four Colchester elections: voting behaviour in a Victorian market town' in K. Newton (ed.), *An Essex Tribute* (Colchester, 1987). The increasing application of computer analysis to pollbooks will no doubt lead to the appearance of further studies in the near future.

Those who wish simply to obtain a broader overview of the period covered could turn to a variety of good general texts: E. J. Evans, *The Forging of the Modern State, 1783–1870* (1983); E. J. Feuchtwanger, *Democracy and Empire: Britain, 1865–1914* (1985) and M. Pugh, *The Making of Modern British Politics, 1867–1939* (Oxford, 1982). Despite its age and brevity, P. Adelman, *Gladstone, Disraeli and Later Victorian Politics* (1970) still has its uses.